WHAT PEOPLE ARE

LEARNING FROM

Jenny Smedley, best-selling author of *Soul Angels*:
"I've known the author for many years and never failed to be impressed on each occasion we've met ... I'd urge anyone seeking to understand their own nature better, or wanting to find ways to improve their life-path, to take advantage of the fact that this inspiring, erudite, and compelling woman has finally put some of her vast, well-researched material into a book."

Sue Lilly, Writer and Spiritual Teacher; Co-Author, *The Essential Guide to Crystals*
"Mary has a knack of being able to explain difficult concepts in terms that are easy to understand, so I was curious to see how she would tackle the issues of time and multiple futures ... In this beautiful book Mary has managed to knit together explanations and techniques so that we can all understand, access and benefit from who we really are. Can't wait to put the techniques into practice!"

Barbara Copperthwaite, Deputy Editor, Full House! Magazine
"The ability to connect with people and explain sometimes complex concepts or emotions in an easy-to-grasp way is not something that comes naturally to many - but it does to Mary. She's an accurate and compassionate intuitive, with a great sense of humour who, despite her great knowledge, is always humble enough to want to learn more. An inspiring person. Full House! readers love her column and her advice!"

Lorna Milton, BBC Radio

"As a journalist, I like fact and hard evidence, and when it comes to matters psychic, I've always been dubious. But Mary Hykel Hunt has won my very sceptical mind around, not to mention those of the listeners of The Lorna Milton in the Afternoon Show on BBC Three Counties Radio, where Mary has been a regular and hugely popular expert on the programme, analysing listeners' dreams and discussing the world of the weird and wonderful in a straightforward and balanced way. I'm convinced! Well, almost ..."

Sir James and Lady Graham, Norton Conyers

"Mary Hykel Hunt wears her learning very lightly and has a great gift for making ancient wisdoms accessible by expounding them in ways which are at one and the same time lucid, useful and practical ..."

Learning from the Future

How to Use Your Future
to Improve Your Present

Learning from the Future

How to Use Your Future to Improve Your Present

Mary Hykel Hunt

BOOKS

Winchester, UK
Washington, USA

First published by O-Books, 2011
O-Books is an imprint of John Hunt Publishing Ltd., Laurel House, Station Approach,
Alresford, Hants, SO24 9JH, UK
office1@o-books.net
www.o-books.com

For distributor details and how to order please visit the 'Ordering' section on our website.

Text copyright: Mary Hykel Hunt 2010

ISBN: 978 1 84694 607 3

A CIP catalogue record for this book is available from the British Library.

Design: Stuart Davies

Printed in the UK by CPI Antony Rowe
Printed in the USA by Offset Paperback Mfrs, Inc

DISCLAIMER

The techniques described in this book are not intended as substitutes for medical or
psychological advice or treatment. Should you suspect or know that you are suffering from
any physical or psychological condition likely to be affected by the practice of visualisation
and/or meditative techniques, it is recommended that you seek medical or psychological
advice before undertaking the visualisations contained herein.

We operate a distinctive and ethical publishing philosophy in all
areas of our business, from our global network of authors to
production and worldwide distribution.

CONTENTS

To My Stone Knight

Acknowledgments

My many thanks to the people who have explored their futures with me and allowed me to mention them. I'd also like to thank John Hunt for his considerable patience and the team at O-Books for their professionalism.

And finally, thanks to my husband Peter for his support, belief and endless supplies of tea and Victoria sponge.

Preface

Learning from the future: a neat, eye-catching turn of phrase, that; a good title for a book, no doubt designed by some marketing sort to grab your attention, because, of course, it's a statement of the impossible. You can't learn from the future, because it hasn't happened yet.

Or can you?

My experience, and that of many people I've worked with in my role as a functioning intuitive and researcher in the field of human consciousness, demonstrates that we CAN learn from the future, quite literally.

Let me be clear about this. I'm not talking about learning from an *imagined* future, something projected from where we are now on the basis of what we know now. Nor am I talking about one of those 'shift in perspective' exercises, so beloved of management training courses, where you look back on the present from some imagined point in the future and ask yourself what it was you did to get yourself out of whatever problem you've currently got yourself into. Nor is it an exercise in simple wish-fulfilment.

No, I'm talking about how we can literally access our future – or rather, our *futures*, since we don't have just one future ahead of us, as this book will reveal – and use that literal information to help us make more informed, more helpful choices and decisions in our present life.

Let me also make it clear that you don't have to don a coin-bedangled headscarf and become proficient in reading a crystal ball or tarot cards to do this. This is most definitely not about becoming Madame Arcati at the end of the pier. Accessing the future is based on good, demonstrable science. Yes, it'll require a considerable shift in your conventional thinking, because reality is not as we see it, as science is increasingly and convincingly revealing. You will meet with some mind-boggling ideas that will leave you feeling as though your brain's been fried. But the payback will be considerable. As you free yourself from the constraints of conventional (and, as will become evident, erroneous) thinking, you'll open up for yourself a whole new universe of possibilities – literally. That's got to be worth a fried brain cell or two.

Chapter One

In the Beginning

I've been an intuitive since I was a child. In fact, I don't remember a time when I didn't see, sense, hear and feel more than other people around me did. Without having to try, I was able to perceive things about the people around me, perceptions that expressed themselves inside my four-year-old head as pictures and symbols. I'd sense things about them – how they felt, things they'd done, things that were going to happen to them in the future.

Names in particular were a great source of information for me. All I'd have to do was hear a name, or see it written down, and straightaway, it would be translated inside my head into an array of coloured geometric shapes and other images that somehow 'spoke' to me, telling me all about the person the name belonged to. I'd get a sense of what kind of person they were, what kind of job they did, whether they were happy, whether they were ill. All kinds of details would come through, including information about their future. In the beginning, I'd tell people about what I was perceiving, but quickly learned that it was better to keep quiet about it, because I invariably got into trouble if I mentioned the things I was picking up.

But I never lost this strange ability. It carried on into my adult life and I know now that, in part, what I'm experiencing is something known as synaesthesia – a condition in which parts of the brain are cross-wired, so that they co-fire in response to a written or verbal stimulus, making it possible to literally hear a colour and see a sound, for example. Complex though my particular form of synaesthesia is, however, it doesn't account for the intuitive output. For that, there has to be another explanation, which we'll touch on later in this book.

Nowadays, as an adult with this kind of ability, I'm regarded as weird but acceptable, in the right quarters, of course. Back in the 1950s, as a four-year old with this kind of ability, I wasn't acceptable in any quarter. I was labelled precocious, different, odd. I compounded my sins by being possessed of a good brain that hoovered up information of all sorts and a photographic memory that retained it all. The synaesthetic/intuitive function enabled me to perceive unusual conceptual links that eventually meant I was also labelled a 'gifted child', without the educational establishment fully realising exactly what my gift was. And by then, of course, I'd learned it wasn't wise to talk about it. So through my teenage years, I kept my secret. I doubt I could have articulated it anyway. Teaching staff waxed lyrical about my intellectual ability, whilst I sat mutely wondering how I could ever explain what actually went on inside my head.

Inevitably, as I grew up, immersion in the academic world beckoned, and I followed, taking not just one but two degrees, eventually studying psychology in the hope that I'd start to find out how people like me operated. This was not the best place to go, as it turned out, at least not initially. In science, orthodoxy rules, and anything pertaining to the psychic or the anomalous is largely regarded as nonsensical, blatantly barmy or just plain deception. The idea that such experiences could be in any way real generally doesn't even get a toehold in conventional scientific thinking, because they just don't fit the rules. Mention that you can glean accurate information about people and situations and the future by means of images and internal voices, and the psychological/medical establishment reaches for the straitjacket and the lithium. So once again, I found myself beyond the pale. Once again, I stopped talking about what it was like to live my kind of life.

But I didn't stop searching for answers. I wanted to understand how people like me could do what they do. Finding myself embodying a kind of interface between the intuitive and the scientific, I began to conduct my own research into the reality and nature of intuition and psychic function. That they were real wasn't in doubt for me, but anecdotal evidence was never going to be enough to convince the world, especially the scientific world. Fortunately, my scientific training gave me some rigorous tools and some good ideas to work with and test it, and I quietly carried on my own private work.

One of my main threads of interest at this time was altered states of consciousness and what could be achieved with them. I was fascinated by what appeared to emerge from the unconscious when people worked in semi-trance states and how the deliberate use of imagery and symbol seemed to facilitate creativity and problem-solving, even, in some cases, physical and emotional healing. I began evolving different techniques with the potential to work more effectively with people in these states. And it was whilst working with a particular client during this stage that I stumbled on the discovery that was to change everything for me.

Joe's Story

Joe was a client who regularly came to see me for intuitive advice and guidance. He'd bring what I'd come to call the usual questions and concerns. But this time was different. This time, he'd brought with him a kind of desperation, a feeling so strong it was possible to feel it sitting in the room with us. He felt he'd hit a kind of wall in his life around his work. He knew he didn't want to carry on with his present job, but had no idea what to do instead.

'So that's why I made this appointment. I just know there's something I'm supposed to be doing – I can feel it calling me, almost. But I've no idea what "it" is. Maybe you can see it?'

He had good reason for asking me that last. I'd built a reputation over the previous ten years on the back of my ability to apparently perceive the future with some accuracy. I say 'apparently' because it wasn't as simple as that – it never is. What I perceive is never a simple or single outcome. Over the years, I'd come to realise that there's no such thing as one fixed future for anyone. Instead, what I perceive as I look ahead is a network of possibilities, based on the choices and decisions each person can make. I call this my 'binary theory of the future' because, just as a computer operating system chooses between a 1 or a 0, we are constantly choosing a yes or a no. 'Yes, I'll take that job/No I won't.' 'Yes, I'll stay in my marriage/No, I'm getting divorced.' With each yes/no choice we make (and a "Don't Know" counts as a "No", since it involves no change), we give rise to another set of choices, another set of possibilities. If I say 'Yes' to that job, I create a new set of possibilities. I meet new people, work in a new environment, maybe even move house – more choices, more possibilities.

And so we make our futures. And the choices and decisions don't have to be mighty ones. They can be simple, everyday choices we make without even giving it much thought. Think Gwyneth Paltrow in the film *Sliding Doors*; in one version of her life she turns left and triggers one set of events and in the other version she turns right, setting in motion a different series of happenings. All of the events that follow in her life are affected by that one simple action of turning one way or the other.

My job as an intuitive is to detect that choice path, and I do this using something I call 'Looking down the Timeline'. When I look down what I call a person's 'Timeline' in response to a question about his or her future, I sense the range of possibilities available at that point, ranging from 'most probable' to 'least likely'. I perceive these 'possibilities' as literal lines extending horizontally out from behind the person and varying in thickness.

The 'most probable' line is always on the person's left and looks as though it's been drawn in with a thick felt tip pen. The 'least likely' is always on the person's right, and looks as if it were drawn with a thin mapping pen. As many lines appear in between as there are possible responses to the question, at least as far as the client is concerned. These lines become thinner the further to the right they appear. As I look at the lines, I become aware of what they mean and can 'see' or sense events along the lines, which can also give me a sense of timing.

As I said earlier, working with this 'network of possibilities' has helped me to realise that there's no such thing as a fixed future for anyone. And nor should there be, because what room would there be otherwise for the notion of free will? Just like Ms Paltrow's Everywoman character, we weave and re-weave our futures daily, hourly, by the minute, with every choice and decision we make, with every choice and decision counting, even apparently mundane choices.

Let's take an everyday example, such as choosing whether to have Weetabix or cornflakes for breakfast. You decide on cornflakes, but it's the last of the box and so later that day, on your way back home from work from the job you dislike, you pop into your local supermarket to buy some more cornflakes. At the checkout, you bump into an acquaintance you've not seen for a while who, during the conversation casually mentions that there's a vacancy coming up at her place of work. You decide to apply and get the job. Voila! Life changed.

Now, would that have happened if you'd decided to have Weetabix that particular morning? Perhaps, but not in the way it did. You'd have given rise to a different future, a different set of choices. And that for me is the essence of free will.

When I'm working with a client, I may see them making a particular choice, but thereafter s/he might then make a different decision, thereby altering the future I'd initially perceived as 'most likely', and bringing in one of the other possibilities. This is as it should be, if free will is to be accommodated. Weetabix or cornflakes? Your choice. Just remember that

7

you're going to be creating a different future with whatever choice you make, even the apparently innocuous ones.

But the question Joe had brought with him this time seemed to be demanding a different approach from my usual 'TimeLines'. This wasn't the commonplace 'I want to change my job' query, because it carried with it a deeper, more urgent kind of energy. Joe was experiencing some kind of calling, or so it seemed to me. And as I sat contemplating him and his problem, I had what I call a Monty Python moment – a metaphoric moment that feels as though the top half of my head is being opened on a hinge, and an idea drops in, whole and complete, without me having to think about it at all. If the 'network of possibilities' idea was true, why couldn't Joe search his own future? After all, plenty of people did past life regressions. I'd assisted many clients to access past lives, to good effect. Might it not be possible to go forward?

When I explained what I was thinking to Joe, he agreed to try.

What resulted was astonishing.

Following my directions, Joe quickly achieved a light trance state and found himself standing at a crossroads with a number of roads leading off it. He sensed one of the roads 'calling' him, as he put it, and started to imagine himself walking along it. After a minute or so, he became aware of a figure walking along the road towards him. This image was glowing, golden, and greeted Joe with real pleasure, telling him that he was Joe from five years ahead. Joe's tone as he related this to me was surprised and sceptical, a situation which didn't improve when I encouraged him to talk to this Future Self and ask what he was doing five years up ahead. Joe's Future Self was quite happy to answer, and told him that he'd decided he wanted to go back to study. He wanted to work in woodcraft and sculpture and had found a university with a course that did just that. He gave Joe not only the name of the university, but also the title and reference number of the course.

As the session continued, I had a strong sense that something important was happening. When Joe resurfaced, he met my excitement with dry scepticism. How on earth could he – or his so-called Future Self – know that information? He was inclined to dismiss it all as fanciful, but I encouraged him to check it out and he said he would. A few days later, a shell-shocked Joe rang to tell me that, yes, that university did offer that course – with exactly that reference number. And that, once he'd recovered from the shock, he'd be applying for the course.

Joe wasn't the only one left with something to think about from that experience. I knew past life regression was possible, having experienced it myself and facilitated it for others. I also knew how helpful it could be in healing present problems. But what had happened here? Had Joe really met himself from the future? It was possible that Joe had accessed future information precognitively. Had we done a Future Progression, as opposed to a Past Life Regression? If so, what other uses might this approach have? And how did it work?

Eileen's Story
Realising I needed to explore this further, I started offering this new approach to other clients, and Eileen, a youthful sixty year old, jumped at the chance. She too had been a regular client, and this time had come with a deep-rooted problem to do with her family. A widow for some years, she'd felt great responsibility for her grown-up children, who always seemed to be in some kind of trouble, whether financial or connected to relationships. She was constantly giving them substantial hand-outs or giving up her time to take care of her grandchildren – often while their parents went off on holidays and other jollies, spending money they didn't have. She'd begun to feel taken for granted and a little resentful, but didn't think she could stop supporting them.

She was keen to try Future Progression. Remembering what had happened with Joe, I suggested to Eileen once she was in a light trance that she find herself at a crossroads. Without any further coaching, she 'saw' several paths leading away, and went for the one that seemed to exert the greatest draw. The path she took led her into in a fairytale wood, Grimms Brothers' style: dark and intimidating. Feeling lost and a little anxious, she became aware of a little old woman coming towards her, dressed in tattered rags and carrying a bundle of firewood on her bent old back; again, a figure straight out of Grimms'. Eileen asked her if she was her Future Self. Eyeing her suspiciously, the old woman said she was. Eileen was puzzled. If this was her Future Self, what did it mean? In a weary voice, the old woman said, 'I represent what you will become if you don't change your ways. And it won't take that long.'

Seeing Eileen's distress at this response, I encouraged her to come back to the crossroads, and this time, to ask to be shown the path that would lead to her own highest good, as well as that of her offspring. Along this second road, she met a well-dressed, confident woman, who told her that when she had been where Eileen was now, she'd decided to start doing some of the things she'd always wanted to do – which included letting her house and buying a Winnebago. Emerging from the trance, Eileen told me that when she was young, she'd always wanted to go travelling in a motor home – a wish that over the years had got buried beneath the demands of family and responsibility. At the end of the session, she left, determined to do something about her life. The next time I saw her, she'd let her house, bought the motor home and was planning a trip with a friend. She had also told her over-dependent and under-industrious offspring that they needed to start taking care of themselves, to their considerable surprise.

Once again, I had some serious thinking to do. Joe appeared to have seen into his future, where he'd been given specific information that he'd been able to verify and then act on. Eileen too had been shown the future, only this time it was a possible future – a future she could change, if she wished.

What was going on? Were these experiences simply coincidental? Were they images rising from the unconscious? Or were Joe and Eileen actually accessing possible futures? And if that were the case, what were the implications of that? Could we learn from the future in such a way that we could divert potential disasters?

Chapter 2

Talking Tattwas

If Joe hadn't come out of his experience with factual knowledge from his 'future', it would have been easy to dismiss the experience as a perspective shift – the kind of breakthrough that comes when we look at something from a different perspective, a technique well known in business coaching circles. But Joe had accessed helpful information in an uncanny way, as had Eileen. And so were many others with whom I was using this technique – including myself.

My own first profound experience of accessing a future life came about by accident when I was doing some experimental work with the Tattwas – a set of images found in ancient Indian philosophy and used to symbolise the five elements from which all of life is made up. They are the Red Triangle, known as Tejas, representing Fire; the Yellow Square, known as Prithivi, representing Earth; the Blue Circle, called Vayu, symbolising Air; the Indigo Oval, called Akasha, representing Ether; and the Silver Crescent, known as Apas, symbolising water.

I was learning how to use these images as energy portals or doorways to different states of consciousness, which is usually achieved by first moving into an altered state of awareness and then imagining stepping though one or other of the Tattwa shapes and allowing oneself to travel on an imaginary inner journey in whatever landscape or circumstances present themselves to your inner vision. It reminded me very much of the BBC *Play School* programme so beloved of young children in the UK in the 1980s – 'Today we'll go through... the ROUND window!'

One morning I decided to work with the Silver Crescent. In

retrospect, it's probably more correct to say that the Crescent decided to work with me, because the minute I stepped through it in my imagination, I found myself undergoing a series of experiences that I would never have consciously chosen for myself.

Opening my inner eyes after stepping through the Crescent, I found myself in what looked like the middle of a John Constable painting. I was standing in a country lane, with the sunlight shafting down through the trees, grass growing along the rutted track. I'd have put money on the fact that round the bend in that lane, I'd find a haywain. This was not the landscape I expected to find on stepping through an Eastern portal, and I hesitated, not knowing what to do next.

I needn't have worried, because the next minute, round the bend in the track trotted a white unicorn.

I didn't react too well to this. When I do inner work of this kind, it's usually devoid of the flowery and the fairy tale and I prefer it that way. I don't typically do white unicorns. I tried to dispel it, but the creature refused to budge. Instead, to my discomfort, it crooked its foreleg and bent its horned head to the ground in a kind of salute, and I just knew it was telling me to get on its back. Try as I might, I couldn't get the image to shift, and so in the end, I mounted, muttering about saccharine images, all the while knowing that this was the only way I'd get anywhere on this inner journey.

The unicorn soared up into the sky and flew out to sea, towards a small island. As we flew down towards it, I spotted a castle on some high land. My irritation level increased another notch or seven, because – predictably, as far as this journey was concerned – this was a fairytale castle, an industry-standard Walt Disney classic, duly turreted and pennanted. Not my style at all. And also predictably, it was completely overgrown by thorn bushes and briars, so that access was impossible. Landing, I slid off the unicorn and looked witheringly at it, at which point it just shrugged and then flew off. (How can a unicorn shrug, I asked myself?) He'd clearly done his bit, as far as he was concerned. So where did that leave me? As I stood looking up at the castle, wondering what on earth to do next, a sword suddenly appeared in my hand, and it slowly dawned on me that I was supposed to carve a way through the thorn bushes up to the castle. Reluctantly, and with a very ill grace, I hacked my way up the steps to the entrance of what was clearly the Great Hall. Peering in, I saw there was nothing in the hall except for a stone plinth on which lay a stone knight, clad in the statutory stone chain mail, stone hands clasped on his stone chest.

Once again, it took a while for me to figure out what I was supposed to do next, and even then, I was so disbelieving, I tried to put it off as long as I could. Kiss the knight? You – whoever You were – had to be kidding! Finally, I did it because, otherwise, I wasn't going to get out of this visualisation with anything useful. And yes, of course, he woke up. As he stood up and reached for my hand, I could see he was quite fanciable, which quelled my bad temper somewhat, even when he led me to the doors of the hall, to be met with cheers from crowds of people in mediaeval dress who certainly hadn't been anywhere in sight when I'd had to hack my way through all those thorn bushes earlier. All of which confirmed my belief that, when it comes to practical help, don't rely on fairy tale characters.

The vision started to dissolve and I took that as my cue to come back through the Crescent. As I slowly came to, I found myself wondering what on earth it had all been about. I was usually able to make some kind of connection between my inner journeys and my outer world, but not this time. I hadn't a clue what it meant. The relationship I *was* in was falling apart, and I certainly wasn't looking for another man. Maybe it wasn't about relationships, I thought. Maybe I'd seen a past life as a knight of some kind. Or perhaps it was about protecting myself more – all that armour and stone. I scrabbled for a few possibilities, but came to no meaningful conclusions. I filed it away in my head under 'Mystery Pending' and decided to forget about it.

So, dear Reader, I leave you to imagine how I reacted when some months later, whilst working through a broken relationship, which was, inevitably, throwing my entire life into disruption, I encountered the Stone Knight in the flesh in the real world. Minus the actual chain mail, admittedly, but nevertheless, quite recognisable as the man in my visualisation. On meeting him, my initial instinct was to run away, especially when he started showing a decided interest in me. It was altogether too much for me to cope with at the time. But in time, the Stone Knight was to become my husband and the story of how that came about was directly reflected in the inner journey I'd taken, all that time before. As our relationship developed, I doubted and fought against the romance that I didn't think I could handle or deserved, and it's a tribute to the man that he persisted. On his side, my vision also reflected certain aspects of his experiences, including how he'd been 'turned to stone' emotionally by previous relationships and what my own part in his emotional awakening was to be. There've been a few thorn bushes to hack through, but it's been worth it, and now I might even grudgingly admit to there being something of the fairy tale about the whole thing.

Reflecting some time later on what had happened during this visualisation, I realised that the journey I'd taken through the Crescent had been a heavily symbolic journey into my future, the symbols foreshadowing the events that were to occur over the next year. I also realised, in retrospect, that it would of course have been about emotions and relationship, since the Silver Crescent represents water – the symbol of the emotions and the unconscious. This time, I'd accessed my own future, complete with some very telling imagery, which was not only precognitive, but was to be profoundly helpful to me, once I started paying serious attention to it.

The evidence was piling up. Something very strange was happening and I couldn't ignore it any longer. Was it possible to literally access the future and bring back information that could change the present? Maybe even affect the past?

Chapter Three

What is Time?

Joe's and Eileen's experiences had confounded me, as had my own. I just couldn't stop thinking about what had happened and its implications. The questions kept beating at me. Could we – are we – able to access future lives? If we are, what does that have to say about the nature of time? If, as I believed, numbers of futures are available to us, might we not be able to use awareness of them to help us live more fulfilled lives? Can the future influence the present? Or even the past?

Past Lives

The notion that we live many lives is a commonly accepted idea, and not just by Buddhists. There appears to be good evidence in support of its reality. Some of the most important work in this field was carried out from the sixties onwards by Professor Ian Stevenson of the Department of Personality Studies at the University of Virginia. Described by the Daily Telegraph as 'the world's foremost scientific authority on the study of reincarnation',[1] Stevenson documented more than three thousand cases of children who appeared to have verifiable memories of past lives. Both a rigorous scientist and unafraid to venture into the unorthodox, he assembled an impressive body of evidence that supported the possibility of reincarnation, all largely ignored (unsurprisingly) by mainstream science, much to his frustration.

One such case study centred on Gopal, an Indian boy who, at the age of three, began talking about a life he'd lived in the city of Mathura, 160 miles from where he currently lived in Delhi. He said that he'd been a businessman who'd owned a company called Sukh Shancharak and that he had been shot by his brother. Stevenson's investigations revealed not only that the company existed, but also that, eight years before, one of the company's owners had actually shot his brother, also an owner. Gopal was invited to meet the dead man's family in Mathura, where he recognised people and places known to the dead man, as well as being aware of his attempts to borrow money, which had led to the shooting – a fact that was known only to the family.

This story was typical of the kind of information Stephenson uncovered and his research provides some commanding evidence as to the reality of reincarnation. And there are many other documented cases of past life memories which involve recall of an actual place or person or event that the subject couldn't possibly have known about, but which have later been verified. For example, in her book, *Souls Don't Lie*, Jenny Smedley describes the life she recalls living in England during the seventeenth century. At that time, her name was Madeleine and she was married to Ryan, who, she claims, has reincarnated today as modern day Country and Western singer, Garth Brooks. Under regression, she was able to recall quite vividly the house in Hampshire that Madeleine and Ryan lived in, including its name and location. She referred to the village they lived in as 'Ham-le-doon' (Hambeldon), which was the correct pronunciation for the time, and was able to recall which of the houses in the village used to be the Green Man Inn, although it doesn't look at all pub-like now. She also claimed that a nearby village, which she called Middleton (today's Milton Abbas), was laid out differently from when she knew it back in the seventeenth century, a claim that was verified by a painting hanging in the present day church, depicting the village before it was destroyed and rebuilt on a whim by the then land owner in the late 1700s.

One of the best known writers on past lives is psychiatrist Dr Brian Weiss, author of several books on the topic, including, *Many Lives, Many Masters*, in which Weiss describes his work with a young patient called Catherine, who was suffering from recurring nightmares and chronic anxiety attacks. Under hypnosis, Catherine began to talk about past lives and events that had occurred in them, which seemed to have a bearing on her present day problems. Initially sceptical, Weiss found his belief system having to undergo a radical change when Catherine started talking about what happened in the time between lives, especially when she began coming through with information that related to his own present day life – information that she couldn't possibly have known. To begin with, Weiss admits he was unwilling to go public with his findings, fearing he would be cast out of the psychiatric community. Putting his findings tentatively to the test with other patients, he became more and more certain of the validity of past lives, to the point that he is able to say:

> By now I've helped more than four thousand patients by bringing them back through hypnosis to their past lives, so my sense of shock at the *fact* of reincarnation, if not the fascination of discovery, has worn off.[2]

So it would seem that good, solid, verifiable evidence in support of the reality of past lives is there for the finding. If we accept that we do live many lives, accessing information about previous lives doesn't seem so far-fetched, assuming we can find appropriate techniques for accurately retrieving those memories. But that was just the point, I thought – they would be *memories*. They would be memories of things that *had* happened. Surely we can only remember what's happened in the past? How can we remember what's yet to happen? That would turn time on its head, wouldn't it? Or was it possible to access a future life, just as it was possible to access a past life? My clients and I had certainly seemed to do so.

Was it possible to project consciousness forwards in time, as well as back? What was time anyway? I needed to find out more about this, and so began a fascinating journey that led me, via physics, psychology, philosophy and quantum mechanics, to some very interesting discoveries of the most definitely brain-frying kind.

Classical Time

When I started to investigate the nature of Time, I began to find out that time isn't what we think it is, or at least, it's not as simple as we think it is.

For most of us, our everyday ideas about time are embedded in what's known as classical Newtonian thinking, which tells us that Time exists as a thing in its own right and flows in a nice orderly 'one-way only' direction, with events taking place sequentially within it. We experience events as a straight line of past-present-future and life is governed by the laws of cause and effect. Cause comes first, followed by effect. I hit my thumb with a hammer, it hurts, I swear and a bruise may appear. We can't have an effect followed by its cause, and effect can't influence cause, because cause HAS to come first. I can't develop the bruise first and then swear before I hit my thumb with the hammer. Nor can I influence the degree of force with which I hit myself by developing only a small bruise first. That would be nonsense, wouldn't it? We can't live backwards.

Or can we? Can we be like the White Queen in *Alice Through the Looking Glass* who shrieks *before* she pricks her finger with her brooch pin? Or like Merlin in T H White's *Once and Future King*, who knows the future because he lives backwards in time whilst everyone else lives forwards?

It was with some surprise that I began to discover that there are indeed people who believe that such things might very well be possible – rational, logical scientists among them – and that to even begin to understand this, we have to rethink what we think we know about time. We need to recognise that what we think we know about time is, in fact, a perception. Venture into the worlds of post-modernist philosophy, psychology and physics and you'll find your ideas about time well and truly stood on their heads.

Does Time Exist?

For a start, there are big questions about the actual existence of time. In certain branches of science and philosophy, time is seen as a system of measurement in the sense of a counting activity. For example, it takes 365 days for the Earth to orbit the sun, more or less, but that can be seen as the number of standardised units it takes for that event to happen, and doesn't have to be seen as the passage of time in the sense of forward-moving duration at all.

For influential philosophers such as Kant and Leibniz, time didn't exist, except as an intellectual structure – a construct we've created, by which we order events in our lives. For them and those they influenced, time per se does not exist. Much Post-modernist thinking in psychology supports this, telling us that we live in a world of constructs, of which time is one. Psychologist Susan Blackmore suggests, for example, that our sense of ourselves as a persisting self having a series of experiences is an illusion. Her view is that 'there are parallel, multiple streams that stop and start and join up.' [3]

In other words, there is no continuous flow of time. There are just a series of 'nows' that we persist in thinking of as a joined-up linear sequence, to which we attribute meaning. We're hard-wired to give meaning to our lives, and so we create a storyline which only *seems* to have a forward momentum. According to this line of thinking, life is really a set of random happenings to which we apply the metaphor of a forward-moving straight line, which doesn't exist in reality.

Turning to the world of the physicists, I discovered that they, too, don't think of time like the rest of us. Let's start right at the top with Einstein. His conclusions about time come through very clearly in the words he wrote in a letter to his friend Besso's family at the time of Besso's death:

Now Besso has departed from this strange world a little ahead of me. That means nothing. People like us, who believe in physics, know that the distinction between past, present and future is only a stubbornly persistent illusion. [4]

Other 'believers in physics' agree. According to Paul Davies, Professor of Natural Philosophy at the University of Adelaide,

Physicists prefer to think of time as laid out in its entirety – a timescape, analogous to a landscape – with all past and future events located there together ... Completely absent from this description of nature is anything that singles out a privileged special moment as the present or any process that would systematically turn future events into the present, then past, events. In short, the time of the physicist does not pass or flow.

He goes on to say that we don't actually observe the passage of time:

What we actually observe is that later states of the world differ from earlier states that we still remember,

In the same article, he later points out that,

A clock measures durations between events much as a measuring tape measures distance between places; it does not measure the 'speed' with which one moment succeeds another.[5]

Brian Greene, Professor of Physics and Mathematics at Columbia University concurs. To Greene, Time is nothing more than 'the book-keeper of change. We recognise that time has elapsed by noticing that things now are different from how they were then.'[6]

So, according to the physicists, most of us have got time wrong, then. Time doesn't really exist, not in a linear sense at any rate, which collapses our ideas of past, present and future. At this point, I started to ask myself whether I preferred my brains scrambled or fried? I was having to dismantle some deeply embedded ideas about the nature of time, ideas that were turning out to be just constructs – perceptions, not facts. At the same time (sorry), I realised that, interesting though this line of thinking was, it was theoretic and did nothing to help me understand what had happened with Joe and Eileen or myself, or whether or how it's possible to access the future or even to define 'future'. Time might very well be a jostling of 'nows', devoid of direction, but we still had cause and effect to deal with. At least it set me thinking about time differently and helped me think beyond the 'arrow of time' notion.

It's Not Time as We know it, Jim…
The next area I looked into was the field of consciousness studies, which also seemed to support this idea of time not existing as we understand it. According to Professor Stuart Hameroff, Director of the Centre for Consciousness Studies at the University of Arizona (and many other like-minded scientists), once again, the passage of time is just a perception. To quote Hameroff, 'Consciousness creates time'.[7]

Current research suggests that time may not exist outside conscious awareness and that, as a result, only in conscious experience does it seem that we move forward in time. Some researchers go even further than this and suggest that things can, in fact, move *backward* in time. This idea is so counterintuitive for most of us that we tend to reject it out of hand. I know I did. It just didn't make sense. Dropped eggs don't unsmash; broken glasses don't unbreak; declared wars don't unstart. There's no such thing as a cosmic rewind button.

It eventually dawned on me, however, that it wasn't the reversal of events that was being talked about. There can't be a cosmic rewind button in that sense, because something called the second law of thermodynamics states that the entropy of a closed system – its state of disorder – will always increase. In other (non-scientific) words, ice melts, hot drinks cool, people age, compost heaps rot, cars eventually fall apart, and so on. Things age, degenerate and fall into ever-increasing disorder.

But this wasn't what Hameroff and others were talking about. They weren't so much asking whether we can go back and change the past, as asking whether the past was affected by the future or whether the past depended on the future in some way. What they were uncovering was the possibility that consciousness seemed capable of jumping forward into the 'future', accessing information and bringing it back to the 'present' – which lined up directly with what I was finding out with my 'jumpers into the future'.

And there's a growing body of evidence that suggests that this can happen. To begin with, scientific research at the quantum level seems to support this idea. Take, for example, Professor John Wheeler's modification of the double-slit experiment, known as the delayed-choice design, which describes how photons (fundamental particles of light) seem able to affect their 'past' choices from the 'future'.[8]

This experiment capitalises on the quirky behaviour of individual photons. Fire a stream of photons through a single slit at a photographic plate, and they appear as a regular bell curve. In other words, they behave like particles. But fire a stream of photons through two slits, and they behave like a wave.

Slow the process down and fire photons individually through a single slit and you see the same single curve as before. Now, open both slits and fire the photons at the screen one at a time. Logically, you'd expect to see two single curves produced through each slit, because you'd expect each single photon to go through just one of the slits. But that's just what doesn't happen. What appears on that photographic plate is a *wave pattern* – which means that our individual photons, fired not as a stream but one at a time, went though *both* slits at the *same time*.

So – fire single photons through a single slit and you get a single curve, meaning they behave like particles. Fire single photons through two slits and you get a wave pattern, meaning they behave like waves.

Wheeler used this little peculiarity to go a step or two further with his 'delayed-choice' experiment. Once again, photons are fired slowly, one after the other, at a photographic plate through a screen in which there are two slits. In front of one of the slits is a very fast shutter, which can be opened or closed *after* the photon has gone through the slit but *before* it 'lands' on the screen. The photon is fired at the plate through the screen, with the decision to close or open the shutter being made *after* the photon has gone past one or both slits. What has been observed again and again is that, irrespective of whether one or both slits were open at the point at which the photon passed through the screen (that is, *before* the decision to leave one or both slits open was taken), the resultant pattern on the screen reflected the conditions dictated by the decision. So, for example, let's say our photon travelled through the screen when both slits were open. The decision was then made to close one of the slits. The resultant pattern on the screen would then be a single curve – not the wave pattern we could have expected. In other words, our clever little photon somehow 'knew' after it had gone through the slits that one of them would be closed later and behaved accordingly. It used future information to change the past, or so it would appear.

And as if that's not enough to fry your brain, at the time of writing, John Cramer of the University of Washington is building a complex experiment, in which he hopes to show a signal arriving before it's sent. He's currently working on the Mark III version.

So at the atomic level, at any rate, photons can look into the future and bring it back to the present – and change the past. What about us humans?

Notes/References

1. Daily Telegraph, 12 February 2007
   http://www.telegraph.co.uk/news/obituaries/1542356/
   Professor-Ian-Stevenson.html
2. Weiss, B (2004), *Same Soul, Many Bodies*, Piatkus Books, p2
3. Blackmore, S, (2003), Interview, Philosophy Now, 42, pp20-21
4. Speziali, Pierre, ed. (1972). *Albert Einstein and Michele Besso. Correspondence 1903-1955.* Paris: Hermann, p215.
5. Davies, P (2002), *That Mysterious Flow, Scientific American,* September, p40
6. Greene, B, *The Fabric of the Cosmos*, Penguin, 2005, p225
7. Hameroff, S, *Time, Consciousness and Quantum Events in Fundamental Spacetime Geometry* in: The nature of time: Physics, geometry and perception - Proceedings of a NATO Advanced Research Workshop, held 21-24 May, 2002 at Tatranska Lomnica, Slovak Republic. Edited by Rosolino Buccheri, Metod Saniga, and William Mark Stuckey. NATO Science Series II: Mathematics, Physics and Chemistry - Volume 95. ISBN 1-4020-1200-4. Dordrecht/Boston/London: Kluwer Academic Publishers, 2003. p.77
8. For more on Wheeler's 'delayed choice', see *Quantum Theory and Measurement*, edited by J.A. Wheeler and W.H.

Zurek, Princeton Univ. Press (1983). See also John Archibald Wheeler, *The 'Past' and the 'Delayed-Choice Double-Slit Experiment'*, pp 9–48, in A.R. Marlow, editor, *Mathematical Foundations of Quantum Theory*, Academic Press (1978)

Chapter Four

Time Knows No Tenses

My forays into philosophy and science had thrown up some fascinating information, which had left me grappling with my notions of what Time was, as well as suggesting that, at the quantum level at any rate, either Time didn't exist or it was something that could be manipulated, at least, if you were a photon. But what if you were a human being?

You Don't Have to be a Brain Scientist – But it Helps...

Digging deeper and ranging wider, I came across the work of neurophysiologist Benjamin Libet. His series of experiments on neural timing, begun as long as thirty years ago with patients undergoing brain surgery, suggest that the brain refers information 'backwards in time'.[1] The patient would remain conscious during surgery, with the brain exposed and skull numbed. Libet would then attach electrodes to the exposed cortex and also to the patient's hands, so that he could deliver an electrical stimulus to both brain and skin, which the patient would then experience as a tingling sensation. Libet would then stimulate the left hand, producing tingling in that hand, whilst simultaneously delivering a stimulus to the left cortex, which would result in tingling in the *right* hand. The patient would then be asked to report which had occurred first.

Because of the distance the impulse would have to travel to the brain from the point of stimulation on the hand, it would be reasonable to expect response to the skin stimulation to take longer than the direct cortical stimulation, which could be expected to be immediate. After all, that part of the cortex was being *directly* stimulated; it should be experienced immediately.

But the results were just the opposite. The skin stimulation was reported immediately, and the brain stimulation was delayed. Somehow, the information from the hand was getting to the brain *before* the information from the direct-to-brain stimulus. Libet concluded that the brain was projecting information backwards in time, that is, from the near future back to the present. In other words, the mind/brain was going forward 'in time', collecting information about the stimulus and bringing it back. The mind/brain was ahead of events. Thirty years later, Libet's findings are still generating a lot of contentious debate, as scientists argue over what they really mean. For Libet, his findings had serious implications as to the nature of free will. If the unconscious was getting hold of information and acting on it before the conscious mind, where did that leave conscious free will?

But for me, this was a real treasure of a find. What if Libet's patients were somehow reading the future and fetching it back? Here was possible evidence that our minds/brains were capable of seeing into the future, even if only by a matter of seconds. It wasn't reversing time – smashed eggs weren't unsmashing – but it was the beginning of a suggestion that we somehow see 'ahead' and 'reflect back.'

And I was even more excited when I discovered Dean Radin's experiments with precognition.[2] Radin, currently Senior Scientist at the Institute of Noetic Sciences in California, is a long-term pioneer in research in this field, and back in the late 1990s, whilst based at the University of Nevada, he designed a series of experiments to look at unconscious precognition, based on physiological responses. A volunteer sitting in front of a computer screen would be asked to cause a picture to appear on the screen by pressing a button. The pictures were a mixture of neutral or emotive images and would be randomly selected and presented to the volunteer by the computer. The volunteer could have no conscious advance knowledge of which kind of image was to be displayed. The participant was 'wired' for response by having electrodes attached to the palm of his or her hand. These measured the physiological responses of the volunteer – skin conductance, blood pressure, heart rate. Once the volunteer pressed the button, a random picture would appear after a five second or so delay and the participant's physical response recorded.

The volunteers responded as expected after being shown the pictures. A neutral image would elicit a neutral response; a powerfully emotive image would produce agitation or arousal. But more importantly from my perspective, Radin also discovered that volunteers were consistently registering the appropriate response *before* they had seen the image. The odds against this being a chance result in this particular experiment were 500 to one – a highly significant result. Somehow, it seemed, people were looking into their futures.

This phenomenon was also being discovered in the work of the Global Consciousness Project, headed up by Roger Penrose of Princeton University.[3] Using random number generators (RNGs) located around the world in various universities and research institutions, the project monitors the RNGs' output for evidence of mind-matter interaction, in particular whether mass attention can influence the data generated by the RNGs. This would be identified by the RNGs suddenly producing non-random output. Results so far suggest that there is such a link, clearly demonstrated in output over the period of time leading up to Diana, Princess of Wales' funeral, as well as that during the funeral of Pope John Paul II. The pattern of unexpected order also appeared at the time of the terrorist attack of 9/11. Even more significantly from my point of view, the data shows that a significant change appeared in the output *two hours before* the first plane crashed into the World Trade Tower. Was this global presentiment? It's a tempting speculation.

I also discovered that interest in visiting the future isn't just the province of scientists. An article in the New York Times on 28 July 2009, entitled 'Hunches Prove to be Valuable Assets in Battle', revealed that US troops were the focus of a study investigating how some soldiers could pick up on danger and take appropriate action, even though there were no obvious signs of it.[4]

As I uncovered more and more research evidence that lent support to the idea of learning from the future, I kept asking myself why none of this information was more mainstream. It was hardly ever reported in the media, and when it was, it was either given the sensationalist treatment or dismissively described as verging on quackery. This struck me as decidedly unfair, since much of it satisfied the exacting conditions that a robust scientific approach demands. One of the gods to be appeased in the world of science is the Great Lord of Replication. In mainstream science, if, after bringing critical judgment to bear on it, other scientists can repeat your work, then it's usually recognised that you're onto something. It's called peer review. Radin's experiments have been replicated again and again, by Dick Bierman of the University of Amsterdam and many other scientists using different methodologies, but despite their high statistical significance, their results and their implications have been largely ignored or rubbished by mainstream science.

Notwithstanding this inexplicable refusal of mainstream science to even acknowledge such findings, I was excited to discover that there was an established and ever-growing body of evidence that suggested that we are somehow capable of accessing information from the future. Admittedly, these experiments show us only going forward by seconds. But at least it was a start. Aside from wondering why these results hadn't hit the headlines and been taken seriously, I also wondered how we were accessing this future information. What mechanisms were we using? What theory might explain this phenomenon?

Radin and others rode to the rescue once more, bearing aloft the concept of quantum entanglement as a possible – indeed likely – explanation for what was clearly happening. It certainly made sense to me, in terms of my own personal experience of sensing the future. Quantum mechanics demonstrates that, at a fundamental level, everything in the universe is connected. Go far enough down into the fabric of the universe, to the microscopic level, to the atomic level, to the spacetime level, and we find a world of strange relationships and apparently paradoxical facts, where an atomic object can be in two or even 3,000 places at the same time, known as superposition; where an object can be both a wave and a particle at the same time, only deciding to become one or the other when observed, or perhaps when it reaches a critical point and collapses; where an object, once connected or **entangled** with another, will instantaneously display an identical response to stimuli applied to the other, however far apart they might be. This is what Einstein described as 'spooky action at a distance' and incidentally did his level best to disprove, because it didn't fit with his theories. An unsuccessful attempt, it must be said, because all it did in the end was prove that quantum theory was correct.

Until recently, most scientists thought that these discoveries operated only at the atomic level. But recent research suggests that quantum phenomena do indeed seem to percolate up to the macroscopic level – to the level of our life experience. For example, current research suggests that quantum mechanics may have something to do with photosynthesis,[5] the sense of smell[6] and even the flu virus.[7] And Radin argues that if we do live in an entangled universe, then so-called paranormal abilities would be an unavoidable consequence, since everything would be connected, a view that Hameroff isn't afraid to espouse either.[8] So my mind can be entangled with that of another and voila! – telepathy, or clairvoyance. And maybe my present self can be entangled with another's future self, hence precognition. And most interesting for me, maybe my present self is entangled with my future self, hence my ability to see my future. Or should that be my present self is entangled with my future *selves*?

One school of quantum thought, called the Multiple Worlds theory, suggests that every superposition branches off and creates a new universe, so that every possibility exists. This idea fits so neatly with what I actually perceive when I look at the future – that network of possibilities that I perceive, which I mentioned earlier – that I'd like to think it's true.

So what had I discovered on this brain-cell frying journey?

Time Knows No Tenses

Firstly, time isn't what we think it is. It's a construct, a product of our conscious awareness, through which we only **seem** to experience time as passing. Simply put, Time knows no tenses. There's no such thing as past, present, future. There's only now, a point when all things are happening, which is why we can access them, once we break out of the idea of straight line time. Time's arrow is an illusion and once we remove the constraints on our thinking about Time, we break out of a prison we didn't know we were in, and with that freedom, other things – outrageous things – become possible.

The Problem of Language

Of course, so embedded is this idea of Time as linear, it's extremely difficult to disengage from it, especially since our everyday perceptions seem to support it. Inevitably, those perceptions shape the language we use to talk about time, and then of course, our language reinforces our perceptions. We talk of going back to the past and ahead to the future, even when we know different. Indeed, it's very difficult to write about time differently in an everyday sense, simply because we haven't yet got to grips with the way it really is. We're wedded to the notion of duration, of time elapsing. Entropy – the rule that says every-thing must eventually degenerate into chaos and breakdown –

supports this illusion, again because we infer the elapse of time. And of course, we can't reverse events – yet. Cause still brings about effect, not the other way round – well, so far, anyway. We still have that interesting experiment of John Cramer's to come yet. But still, I don't need to infer from the results of entropy and the play of cause and effect that time is linear. Brain frying though it is, I can (just about) conceive that the only place time exists is in my mind, as a matter of perception.

Real Evidence

What I'd discovered is that we can be misled by our everyday perceptions, that they can and do limit us, and that experimental evidence exists that time is otherwise than we think it is. Most importantly, we have substantial clinical evidence that we can and do 'see the future', mostly unconsciously, probably on an everyday basis, as Radin's and Libet's work has convincingly illustrated.

The evidence so far shows us accessing only small amounts of information from what we construe as 'a little way ahead'. That's probably why we don't recognise it as such and, remember, we're talking about **unconscious** precognition here anyway. That's a long way from what I'm talking about – accessing a full-on future experience from some years 'ahead' (or maybe it's sideways, if the Multiple Parallel Universe theory turns out to be right) and using the information to inform our 'present'. But might this not be the preliminary evidence that leads on to more research into whether or not we can go further? Why stop here?

One thing I knew for certain was that here were some possible explanations for what was emerging for my clients and myself. Maybe we were literally 'visiting the future', popping next door into a parallel dimension to see how things turned out there. For the first time, I felt a sense of hope. What I and my clients were experiencing wasn't being dismissed by others as another brand of weird. There were others out there looking at the same things I was, and taking it seriously – and I was in good company.

Notes/References

1. Libet, B (2004), *Mind time: The temporal factor in consciousness*, Perspectives in Cognitive Neuroscience, Harvard University Press
2. Radin, D, (2006), *Entangled Minds*, Paraview Pocket Books, New York
3. As well as Radin's book mentioned above, see www.noosphere.princeton.edu/ for information on the Global Consciousness Project. See also Nelson, R, (2009), *Is the Global Mind Real?*, EdgeScience, The Society for Scientific Exploration, 1, pp 6-9
4. See EdgeScience edition referred to above, p 15, for commentary
5. See *Evidence for wavelike energy transfer through quantum coherence in photosynthetic systems*, Engel et al, in Nature **446**, 782-786 (12 April 2007)
6. See Turin, Luca (1996). *A Spectroscopic Mechanism for Primary Olfactory Reception. Chemical Senses* (Oxford Journals) **21**: 773–791. http://chemse.oxfordjournals.org /cgi/reprint/21/6/773.pdf . See also Brookes, Jennifer C.; Filio Hartoutsiou, Andrew P. Horsfield, and A. Marshall Stoneham (2007-01-16). *Could Humans Recognize Odor by Phonon Assisted Tunneling?. Physical Review Letters* (APS) **98** (038101): 038101.
7. See *Toward quantum superposition of living organisms*, Romero-Isart, O et al in *New Journal of Physics* **12** (March 2010)
8. See Hameroff's discussion with Alwyn Scott in Carter, R, (2002) 'Consciousness', p 298 ff

Chapter 5

Fetching Your Future

The build-up of experiences around what I was starting to call Future Progression convinced me that it worked. I kept trying it out with different clients and found that it produced different results depending on the client's context. Every 'inner journey' was different. But I soon realised that there were certain key essential points to every 'journey', and a fundamental pattern began to emerge.

Over time, I've built this pattern into a protocol that people can use by themselves, without having to do anything complicated. All that's needed is a quiet place, sufficient time and a reason for doing it. And experience has also shown that almost everyone is quite capable of interpreting their own symbols and experiences. And why shouldn't they be? After all, the symbols and experiences are organic. Even if they don't yield understandable information immediately, understanding seems to come through later.

Using this protocol is also useful, in that it turns the process into a ritual – not a formalised one, nor one that necessitates the sacrificing of goats or virgins, but, nevertheless, a ritual. Formal though this term sounds, there's a useful idea behind it, namely to send a signal to the unconscious mind, telling it to prepare for a specific kind of work – that a different state of consciousness is expected. Think about what happens to most of us when we enter any kind of sacred space, whether it is a church, a mosque or an ancient stone circle. Something shifts within us. We recognise we're in a place different from the everyday and we open up to the possibility of communication beyond the normal. That's the point of the protocol. A way of preparing that sends a signal to the unconscious to ready itself for something different, for elevation to a different level of communication.

Using this protocol also gives a structure to the process. This is not a rule-bound structure, which would be likely to hamper spontaneity (and anyway, the subconscious doesn't like rules much – or at least, only the ones it decides on), but a structure based on sound psychological and spiritual practices. Structure makes self-delusion less likely, as well as preventing the whole thing just becoming a 'stream of consciousness' type exercise, which, whilst undoubtedly fascinating, would be likely to yield little directly relevant information – rather like using a fishing net that caught every type of fish, rather than one designed for the specific fish you were after. The protocol is designed to elicit images and symbols (which in my experience usually have enough to say for themselves anyway) that are organic to the person and her/his questions.

Protocol: The Preliminaries

Note: you'll find that what follows is peppered throughout with descriptions of time that imply it's linear. This is for ease of communication and understanding. As indicated elsewhere in this book, so embedded is this notion of time that it would be self-defeating to present people with new concepts that would be distracting whilst in the middle of a deep process such as this is. Asking someone to think of their Future Self as inhabiting a parallel dimension would be likely to distract them from the task at hand. For most people, it's hard enough to grasp that they could even meet themselves in the future, let alone a sideways one.

You need to choose a quiet, comfortable place to work where you're not likely to be interrupted. Allow at least half an hour for the process. Turn off the phone and have a glass of water near by, together with a pen and some paper. You also need to think about from how far ahead you want your Future Self to be. Experience has shown that it's better to choose a time at least a year or more ahead, at least to begin with, as too close a time scale doesn't offer a sufficient enough difference to be useful. It's also better not to go too far ahead, as the results tend to be too broad. The usual time frame chosen is three or five years ahead.

Experience has also shown that your Future Self may not be just an older version of you. In fact, it's extremely unlikely to be. People have met themselves as mythical images (such as Merlin or Gandalf), as animals (wolves, rabbits), as energy states (balls of energy, flashes of light), as vibrant colours, as cartoon characters – the list of possibilities is endless. I've had a deeply meaningful conversation with myself as a rusty tin bucket, as well as Donkey from the cartoon *Shrek*, to name but two. The way your Future Self presents is highly significant and can yield all sorts of interesting insights in its own right. (And yes, Donkey was about being stubborn.)

You'll find that the protocol suggests that you see where you are now – your 'present' – as a place where roads or paths converge – a crossroads. This image has spontaneously emerged so often in my work with clients, as an image of their 'present', that I came to the conclusion that it must be a part of the collective unconscious and decided to incorporate it into the protocol. That it should emerge so often isn't surprising, on reflection; the crossroads or crossing place has long been an image associated with access to other dimensions; it's an image that conveys choice of direction – where do I go now? Sometimes, helpful signposts or road signs are present in the image. These signs don't always contain words, it has to be said. Often, the sign carries a symbol, which may take a bit of decoding. But if none of this appears in your imagery, don't be concerned. One client found herself in the middle of a river and just 'went with the flow'. Others have just seen themselves as the convergence point, with the roads or paths flowing out of themselves. For variety's sake, an alternative script can be found in the Appendix.

This is essentially a visualisation process or, as I prefer to call it, an imaging process. Some people claim that they can't do this, but if you can daydream, you can 'visualise'. I must rank among the world's worst imagers, because all I usually get is just a whisk of an image – but it's enough. I know what it is, and I can work with that. It may be the same for you. You may not literally see anything at all, but this is likely to be because you sense or feel your images and just 'know' what's there. Don't struggle to make yourself see something in your mind's eye if it doesn't work that way for you. You do not have to see every little detail, feel every little step. Remember, it's like daydreaming. Equally, don't get hung up on hearing what the images have to say to you. Frequently, you'll just 'know' what they're saying without hearing words spoken or seeing them speak. It comes as a surprise to many to realise that images don't have to move their mouths to communicate, and that all you have to do is be open to feeling what they are conveying.

The Questions

Now's the time to think about what you want to explore. Just sit quietly and allow yourself to imagine the following:

Imagine that your Future Self from five years ahead (or however many years ahead you wish to go) actually walked into the room where you are right now. There s/he is, standing in front of you. What would be the first thing you'd want to ask? What would you want to know?

At this point, it's quite usual to do go blank, especially on the first occasion. It's so unlikely a scenario that most people don't have an immediate response. So give yourself some time to think about this. Suspend your disbelief and let yourself imagine what it would be like to *really meet* your Future Self. What questions would be top of your list? Your response is going to be highly subjective and individual, so these questions will be different for everyone.

However, I always encourage my clients to come up with some *specific* questions, because experience has shown that this produces more useful results. In fact, the 'quality' of your questions tends to dictate the quality of your outcome. Your questions will obviously depend on what you've set this meeting up for, and this can be about anything. Just remember, general questions generate general answers. So avoid vague questions, such as 'Are you happy?' *Of course* you'll want to know if the Future Energy you're communicating with is happy. But how did they get to be happy? What did they have to go through to get there? Is their particular future all it's cracked up to be? Were there other, better choices?

And don't ask closed questions. 'Did you get that contract?' is an example of a closed question, because all it invites is a 'yes' or a 'no' response. It doesn't invite your Future Self to expand on its answer, which can then lead into something of an interrogation. This is hard work and not necessarily very productive. You want your Future Self to talk freely and without too much prompting. Much better to ask something like, 'What happened then?' and give your Future Self the opportunity to talk about its experiences.

You can use this technique to enquire about anything. Remember, Joe's question was about his career, Eileen's about her family, mine (inadvertently) about relationship. One client I worked with wanted to buy a house and settle down, after a long period of semi-nomadic existence spent shuttling between different members of her family as a carer. She'd found a house she wanted to buy and decided to check it out with her Future Self from three years ahead. Had her Future Self bought the house? she asked, confident of the answer. To her present day self's initial surprise, her Future Self told her, no, she hadn't. After thinking about it, she (her Present Self!) realised that there were some problems with the property that she'd been ignoring, so keen was she to buy a house – any house – and settle down.

Such were the problems that they would have had a big impact on the work that she wanted to do from home, had she gone ahead. So she decided to wait a while longer for the right property to crop up, as guided by her Future Self. At the time of writing, she's happily settled in the house she finally bought in the Findhorn Community Ecovillage.

It's useful to do this preliminary think, because it primes your subconscious. If you'd like to and it helps to focus, write your questions down. As you undergo the Future Progression, the questions then usually arise quite naturally. However, there is one very important point to remember: don't be superficial about this. Your questions need to be issues you really want answers to. Don't go into this process in an unthinking way, or out of idle curiosity, because it's unlikely to produce worthwhile results. The emotional charge of your questions seems to be important, as there does appear to be a direct relationship between that charge and the quality of the answers you get.

And whilst talking about 'emotional charge', it's important that you don't go into this process in a state of desperation or fear, because both these energies will distort your experience. You'll end up getting in your own way. If you are feeling this way, the opening part of the process, which is all about relaxing in order to achieve an altered state of consciousness, will help you let go of your fears and feelings of desperation – but you do have to give yourself permission to let go.

One more point: don't even **think** about using this approach to gain information about others that you have no right to, or to manipulate others.

What if it happens differently from what I'm suggesting?
If things go differently from the way I suggest, go with what's happening for you. This point is important. This is *your* experience, based on *your* intuition, *your* psychic data. Interfere with this, and you'll get a meaningless outcome, as Donald's

experience illustrates. Donald's main problem was that he was lazy, and always wanted someone else to do the work for him, especially when it came to inner work. So all he did was follow my suggestions, without checking them against his own internal reality. As a result, what happened had no authenticity and it didn't work. If whatever is suggested doesn't feel as though it belongs to you, then it doesn't. Go with what is coming through for you, and ignore the protocol, which is, after all, only a guideline. If I'm suggesting you find yourself on a beach and you're on top of a mountain, STAY THERE and go with what happens!

My client Helen's experience is a good demonstration of this. She'd come with a career question and I'd started the session off with my well-practised opening speech about crossroads and signposts. Halfway into it, she stopped me and said, 'There aren't any roads. Or paths. I'm in the middle of a river. I'm standing on a small rocky outcrop in the middle of this big, slow-moving river.' I recognised straightaway that she was in control of her own visualisation, and I stopped waxing lyrical about paths and signposts. Instead, I started asking prompting questions about where she was, encouraging her to tell the story of what was happening to her. The journey she went on involved her diving into the river and letting it take her forward to the meeting with her Future Self. The experience was viscerally powerful and what she learned from that meeting is still playing out in her present life. So much more was achieved because I shut up and let go. So once again – go with your own experience and don't try to force it to fit someone else's expectations, because it won't work.

One more thing to learn from Donald's experience was that he convinced himself that he only had to do this journey once, and that would be it – future sorted. I had to work hard to disillusion him of this idea. Future Progression is meant to give you access to guidance and advice, not just once in your life, but many times over. There are so many choice points in our lives, a one-off Future Progression could never provide answers for all of them. So, if Future Progression works well for you, be prepared to use it again and again.

How do I know it's real and I'm not just imagining what I want?

When you're using Future Progression, don't let yourself be fooled by your own wish-fulfilment fantasies, or by your feelings of fear and depression. Neither will help you. The whole point of doing the Future Progression is to meet with real answers, real solutions.

How do you stop yourself fooling yourself? You *feel* its reality. There's a qualitative difference between a *real* image and an *illusory* one. The best way I can describe it is that a real image has substance and weight to it, and is quite likely to argue with you and point out where you're going wrong. But it'll be constructive, not destructive.

An illusory image will present in two possible ways. It can feel like candy floss – sweet and lacking in substance – in which case, it will offer no resistance and tend to come up with inane responses, such as, 'You'll succeed,' without telling you how or giving you something concrete to work on. The other possibility is that it will present in a negative, down-pulling way, telling you you're no good, leaving you feeling there's no way out.

Neither of these types of illusory image will be truth-tellers. They won't serve you, and need to be dismissed. I've evolved a technique to use when I'm in doubt as to whether an image is real or not, and that's to ask it simply: 'Are you real?' If it's not, the image just dissolves. If it is, it stays.

What if you're shown something you don't like?

On these inner journeys, anything can happen. They frequently won't often follow the nice, neat pattern I'm about to describe. I'd be very surprised if they did, since, after all, we're dealing with your unconscious, which doesn't tend to pay attention to any rules, and certainly not the rules of logic.

If you're exploring future possibilities, it's quite possible that you'll be shown something you don't like. If that happens – if you're shown a future that scares you witless or threatens to bury you in boredom – *remember you can change it*. You still need to pay attention to it, because the experience is telling you something about your present life – probably something that you need to change.

What if you don't see a future?

By this, people usually mean they're worried they've died. Very occasionally, they even think they've seen their deaths.

Let me be clear here. I've never yet seen this occur in this process. Yes, we all die eventually, but if it is *ever* communicated in this process, it's unlikely to be represented as something dark or fearful. Dark images are much more likely to represent either *fear of the future*, or a *current unhelpful behaviour*, rather than impending physical death. If you encounter a dark or frightening image, first remind yourself that you're protected, and then *talk to the image.*

Remember Eileen's experience all the way back in Chapter One? On her first path, her Future Self emerged as a bent old woman dressed in rags, carrying a bundle of firewood on her back. Taken aback, Eileen asked whether she was her Future Self, and the old woman replied that she was what Eileen would become if she didn't stop giving her dwindling savings to her indolent grown-up children. Eileen didn't like this future, hightailed it back to the convergence point and asked to be shown the future she could have if she heeded the old woman's advice. A brighter future did indeed beckon, which materialised in Eileen's external life – to her great relief!

So, to summarise the preliminaries:

- Set up a time and a place where you'll be comfortable and won't be interrupted for your session
- Have a glass of water and pen and paper nearby
- Choose from how far ahead you'd like your Future Self to be
- Remind yourself that your Future Self is unlikely to be merely an older version of you – some kind of image or symbolic representation is more likely
- Consider your questions – write them down if you like
- Approach it in the most relaxed way you can

Future Progression

The process starts off with a session of deep relaxation. The deeper you can go with this without falling asleep, the better. Ideally you're aiming for what is known as Theta state (where the electrical activity of the brain is between 5 and 8 cycles per second), also known as the meditative state. This state is associated with higher mind functions, such as creativity, intuition, insight and imagery. You then move on to the visualisation section, where you evoke and communicate with images and symbols representing the Future Self. Make sure you give the images time to come in and establish themselves – and remember that you may sense or feel rather than see what's going on. Finally, you move on to the concluding section, which helps you absorb the imagistic answers obtained.

Note: If you record this for your own use, read slowly, observe the pauses and aim to match your own relaxation rhythms.[1]

Make yourself comfortable, sitting or lying down, and close your eyes. Remind yourself why you're doing this and what your questions are.

And now begin by focusing your attention on your breathing ... just focus on your breath, letting your breath gently rise and fall ... noticing the ebb and flow of your breath ... and, at the same time, give yourself permission to relax ... just checking through your body for where you might be holding tension ... letting your jaw soften ... noticing where your shoulders are, and if they're up underneath your ears, just let them relax, and let your arms and hands and fingers become heavy ...

[Pause]

And now just notice how you're holding your upper body ... if you're clamping your muscles around your ribs and shoulder blades, just use your breath to help them relax ... just breath ease and relaxation through your muscles ... letting your ribs relax, and feel each one of them give a little sigh of relief as they let go...

[Pause]

Allow yourself now to become aware of how you're holding your lower body, and again, if you're clamping your muscles around your tummy and lower back, just breathe through them, telling them they can let go for the time being ... and feel that girdle of muscles gently relaxing all the way round, across your abdomen ... and around into the small of your back ...

[Pause]

And now gently bring your attention to the muscles in your legs ... relaxing the muscles in your thighs, just noticing how the rest of the muscles in your legs let go, too ... feel any tension you may be holding in your knees just evaporate ... and let any little knots of muscles in your calves gently unravel ... feeling any tension in your ankles just dissolve away ... leaving your feet and toes feeling warm and heavy ...

[Pause]

And now just allow yourself to sit there for a moment or two ... giving yourself over to the support of the chair or the floor ... feeling yourself being held up by the chair or the floor ... just give yourself over to their support, ... just ... letting ... go ...

[Pause]

Now just imagine that you're floating ... gently floating ... gently floating down, softly falling, just like Alice in Wonderland falling down the rabbit hole ... it's a pleasant experience ... just floating down ... until your feet touch the ground ... you gently open your inner eyes and look around ... and you realise you're in another dimension ... you're standing in some kind of landscape, with a number of roads or paths leading away from where you stand ... Notice how many roads or paths there are, leading away. Notice if there's a signpost in the middle where the roads intersect, and if there's anything written on its arms ... or perhaps there are road signs nearby ... if so, just notice if there's anything written on them. If there is, it may appear in pictures or symbols rather than words, and they may not make any sense to you. Or they may just be blank. Whatever is or isn't there is fine; you're just checking to see if there's something there or not.

Now just imagine you're standing where the roads converge, which represents your present ... look at the paths available to you, and ask to be shown the path or road that will be of most benefit to you to explore on this occasion. One of the roads will draw you ...

[Pause]

And now imagine yourself walking along that path or road. Just notice what's around you. It may be a rural landscape or a path over a mountain top or along a beach, it may be summer or winter, night or day – anything is possible here, so just take the first image you sense or see. Just notice where you find yourself. Notice, too, how you feel being here – are you happy to be here? Do you feel safe? Puzzled? Curious? Again, just accept the feelings you experience ...

[Pause]

Now, look up ahead and see someone or something coming towards you. Let the image become clearer as this entity comes closer. You know this is your Future Self from ...... years hence. As the image draws closer, take in the details. Notice how your Future Self presents, because the imagery will have meaning...

[Pause]

And now your Future Self comes up and greets you, and you respond. This is your opportunity now to talk to your Future Self and to ask the questions you want answers to. Take as much time as you need to do this, allowing your Future Self sufficient time to respond as well, either in words or thoughts or pictures or symbols. If you're confused by anything your Future Self gives you, ask for clarification. Take as much time as you need...

[Pause]

Your time is drawing to a close ... but before this experience comes to an end, just take your consciousness, your awareness, your sense of yourself, and lift it out of you and drop it into your Future Self, so that you are looking back at your Present Self through your Future Self's eyes ... Notice what you see or feel as you look back at your Present Self ... how do you look? ... What do you need? ... Let your Future Self supply the answers to your awareness ... and then allow yourself to come back into your Present Self ...

[Pause]

And there's one more question you might like to ask. **Just ask your Future Self what she or he did when she or he was where you are now.** What was the first step she or he took when they were where you are right now? Allow yourself to hear or feel or sense or just know the answer ...

[Pause]

And now your Future Self has a gift for you ... a symbolic gift that will help you on your way ... again, just take the first image that comes into your head. It can be anything, so allow it to be what it needs to be. If you need more information about it, ask your Future Self to explain it ...

[Pause]

... And now it's time to say your farewells, so thank your Future Self for coming to see you ... and now just allow your Future Self to merge with you ... notice how you feel as he or she steps into you and just melds with you ... really allow

51

yourself to feel this experience ...

[Pause]

And then come back to the place where the roads meet, which represents your present, and look up once more at the road signs, if there are any. Notice if anything is written on any of them. Take note if there is – and if there isn't, that's fine.

Now just start to come back ... allow yourself to start coming back through the different levels of awareness, as though you're a diver, swimming back up slowly to the ocean's surface. Don't come up too fast ... take your time and surface slowly ... slowly coming back to everyday awareness, bringing back with you the memories of what you heard and felt and saw ... slowly surfacing ... until you feel ready to open your eyes ... and are ready to be back, present in this room, at this time, awake and refreshed.

Take a sip or two of water and then make notes on your experience.

The point of giving you the protocol to follow is to help you learn how to do the journey. But essentially, it reduces to just five points:

1. Relax

Relax sufficiently to allow yourself to enter an altered state of consciousness – a pompous way of saying just let yourself go into a daydream state.

2. Allow

Whatever then happens, don't force or direct it. Let the story unfold. If it takes you by surprise, let it. This is not an exercise in wish fulfilment, it's an exploration. You're not trying to make things happen the way you think they should. You're exploring future possibilities.

3. You can change it

If you don't like what's happening and feel it's wrong –

remember you can change it. Take note of it, because the experience is telling you something about your present life – usually something you need to change. Remember Eileen's experience. Just take note of what's emerged – and then bring yourself back to the cross roads and ask to be shown the road you need to travel if you're to avoid the fate you've just been shown – and see what happens.

4. Integrate
You'll notice that at the end, it's suggested that you meld with your Future Self. This anchors the energies of your Future Self in you in the present and usually triggers events and experiences that put you on the right path.

5. Act
There's not much point on doing all of this if you're not going to take any notice of it ...

Now What?
Now's the time to reflect on your experience. You've been working with imagery, and images usually yield more information and insights if you spend some time reflecting on them.

Amongst the things to consider might be the number of roads or paths you saw leading off from the crossroads. This usually indicates the number of choices available to you in your current situation. And were there any road signs? Was there anything written on them? If there is, this can be pretty interesting. One of my signposts simply had *Up*, *Down* and *Level* written on its three arms. I felt I'd been doing *Up* for a long time and was tired and bored with it. *Down* felt as though it would take as much energy as *Up*, and so I chose *Level*, even though it appeared to be just a windy little sheep track. It led me to some extraordinary experiences, however, which are currently manifesting right now in my life as I attempt to make my life less demanding.

Another point to take into consideration is what the paths or roads are like? Are they easy? Rocky? Uphill? Are they roads at all? As we've already seen, they might not be – take Helen's's river, for instance, an image that could have all sorts of meanings, such as 'River of Life' or 'Go with the flow'. One client even had an airport runway leading off from her crossroads, which we eventually realised pointed to the possibility of working and maybe even living abroad. Right next to her runway was a bendy little overgrown path, which represented her thoughts about escaping to the country. Her Future Self met her on the runway, which was the path she eventually took.

And what does your Future Self actually look like? Remember it won't necessarily be an older version of you – in fact, it's most unlikely to be just that. S/he may appear as a ball of light, a shapeless colour, a fairytale character, or a mythical figure – anything is possible. It's likely to be symbolic in nature, and so deserves attention, because it will be telling you something about you and your situation. Take Eileen's bent old woman, for example. This wasn't telling her that she'd literally become a bent old lady living in the forest, picking up sticks for a living. It was symbolic, warning her that she'd become worn out and poverty-stricken, if not financially, then emotionally.

A Future Self I once met presented as Joda, the Jedi Master character in the Star Wars films who lives in a swamp and trains the hero-in-waiting Luke Skywalker to be a Jedi Knight. Thinking I'd met something really good here, I was a bit surprised when he told me I couldn't be both spiritual **and** materially comfortable. It was one or the other. If I wanted to be spiritual, I had to give up life's comforts and go and live in a swamp, so to speak. This wasn't ringing true for me, and as I had no inclination to end up living in an alien swamp, literally or metaphorically, I came back to my convergence point and began again. This time, I met my Future Self in the form of a powerful black horse, glossy-coated, free and untrammelled, self-sufficient, able to go wherever she wanted under her own steam and without being harnessed by anyone or anything. The horse told me how to go about achieving this. Fifteen years later, I'm pleased to report that my life is both spiritually focused and comfortably swampless. I'm also self-employed and powering ahead under my own steam. (The use of an image of a black horse as a well-known logo for a UK bank, thereby linking it with finances, wasn't lost on me either.) It was, however, interesting to reflect on what that Future Self Joda had to say about me and the way I was thinking at the time – and where I might have ended up if I hadn't shifted my way of thinking.

The 'drop-in' of your awareness into the Future Self can also be very telling. It's more than just a perspective shift. Many people are quite startled by what they see when they look back at themselves. Clients have seen themselves as a child, or as small, tired, empty, lost, or tortured, and it can kick-start major change, frequently bringing about an immediate awareness of what needs to happen to improve things.

And then there's the gift. Not much mention has been made of this aspect, but the same rules apply. Joe's gift was the reference number of the course he was going to take. That was a very direct and obvious gift. Sometimes they're less obvious, like the sparkly pink horseshoe I was once given. It looked as though it should belong to Barbie's pony (if indeed she ever had one), and I was sceptical, to say the least, especially since I've never in the slightest been a horsey person – or a Barbie type, come to that. But given the equine imagery overall, it eventually made sense as a magic shoe to help me on my way. Move over, Dorothy – who needs red slippers when you've got sparkly pink horseshoes?

The important thing to remember is that *images communicate*. They can't help it. They always mean something. It's that 'pictures speak a thousand words' thing. Sometimes it may take time before they yield their meaning and, occasionally, you may have to be quite demanding with them, especially if you're asking for further explanation of a symbol. Don't be afraid to push for clarification. If you feel you need further insights, it can be useful to talk it over with someone who won't think your marbles have gone roll-about, but it's worth the wait, so be patient. Insight can often strike when you're busy doing other things. In my case, it's usually when I'm doing the ironing!

And finally, remember that last question I suggested you ask your Future Self? The one that asks what was the first thing s/he did when they were where you are now? Mind-bending though this may seem in a *Back to the Future* sort of way, it's advisable to pay serious attention to the answer you received at that point and to act on it. So much good advice has come through at this point. Remember, this is really your Future Self you're talking to, and he or she has already done what you're about to do, so they know what you did – if you see what I mean. As such, they're qualified to give advice.

Notes and References

    1. A CD of this journey process is available from www.hykelhunt.co.uk

Chapter 6

Using Your Future in Your Present

One of the fascinating aspects of working with your future in this way is the many ways you can apply it. Over the years, I've used it with all kinds of clients in all kinds of situations, and to good and sometimes startling effect.

Finding Direction

It was an ideal tool to use with those who came to see me because they'd lost direction in their life, or who felt they'd arrived at a crossroads and didn't know which way to go. Meeting with a Future Self usually provided insight and guidance that had practical results.

Claire fell into this category. Facing redundancy, she was at a loss as to what to do. Fear was threatening to swamp her, as she faced a future with little money and no prospects. Meeting her Future Self in the form of a gold star, she learned that she'd used some of her redundancy money to retrain as a life coach and had set up her own business, which had proved quite successful – especially as she was able to utilise her old contacts from her previous business world. This just hadn't occurred to Claire in her present context, and off she went to explore the possibilities. Two years later, she was ready to start her business, set fair for success. A Gold Star, helping others achieve or become Gold Stars.

Something similar occurred for Maureen, who just knew she had to leave her present job as a professional nanny before she completely lost it with her employers. They seemed so disconnected from their children that Maureen knew she couldn't stay. One Future Progression later, Maureen was confirmed in her decision, although she still didn't know where to go. Her Future Self appeared as a fairy-like being and told her to put in her three months' notice, and that before the end of the period she would be offered another job. Maureen's response was interesting in that, initially, she found the fairy laughable. How could this be an image of her Future Self, she asked? But she knew the image carried a real message, which she also knew she wasn't getting quite yet. So she decided to put her response on hold, and just wait. Displaying real trust and faith, she didn't even attempt to find another job – and a month before her notice was up, she was offered a better position elsewhere, with better pay, better hours and greater autonomy.

Relationship Questions and Trying Out Different Futures

I discovered that relationship questions could be approached using this method, too. Linda was faced with an age-old dilemma. Involved with a married man for many years, she'd now reached a point where she just didn't know whether it was worth hanging on for him any longer. His reasons for not having yet left what he described as a dead marriage centred round his children. He wanted to wait until they'd all left home and were properly fending for themselves. But after seven years of waiting, Linda could no longer be sure he would ultimately leave, so she wanted to be shown what the future would be like without him, as well as with him.

During a Future Progression around this question, she met two possible futures. In one, the Future Self she met was living alone in an empty house located deep in an empty forest. Nothing was happening in this future life, and it felt pointless. She knew she didn't want this, and so asked to be shown another, better future and what she'd have to do to achieve it. In this, she saw herself with her man, living together in an out-of-the-way place. The happiness she felt at the outset started to evaporate as she watched his grown-up children walking across the field of dreams that surrounded her house. They called their father out and talked to him, apparently asking him to go with them. To her consternation, he went, and thinking that she'd been left on her own again for good and that he'd never come back, she saw herself carrying on with her life. However, shortly after, he came back through the door of the cottage, explaining to her that he'd had to go and sort out a problem for his children. She realised that what she was being shown was that, yes, she could have a life with him – and that life would always include his children, however old they were. She felt that she could accept this, feeling it was the right thing for him to do.

This last example shows how it's possible to explore different potential futures, an approach that can pay off when you're trying to make a decision or choose between two or more options, or are simply stuck. It's possible to talk to your Future Self and ask to be shown what the eventual outcome would be if you took any of the options available – and also to be shown any options you've not thought of. In the world of quantum physics, multiple futures are quite possible, remember, and available for exploration. From this perspective, it becomes possible to choose an appropriate future.

Another area of self-healing that Future Progression can help with is that of emotional healing. Take Pat's case. She'd had a difficult relationship with her mother since childhood. Puzzled and bewildered, she never knew what it was she wasn't getting right as far as her mother was concerned and, unsurprisingly, this uncertainty spilled over into her life generally. She felt she was somehow always in the wrong whatever she did, with inevitable consequences for her relationships and career. Whilst doing some image work with me around this issue, she met her Future Self as a kindly and confident businesswoman, dressed in a red jacket, who gave her a giant eraser and a pencil, with the words, 'No mistake makes you permanently wrong. Rub out what's not true about what others say about you, and write in what *you* know to be true.' As Pat heard those words, the cosmic penny dropped, and she realised that she'd been treating others' opinions about her as though they were facts. She suddenly became aware that much of what she'd been told by her mother about herself as being inadequate and stupid just wasn't true. This realisation was profoundly transforming for her and she was on the way to becoming the confident woman epitomised by the Future Self she'd met.

Getting Unstuck

Linda's example above also demonstrates that our Future Selves don't always require us to work on the basis of blind faith. Sometimes our Future Selves tell us to sit and wait, that we need do nothing to make the future happen, except trust, as in Maureen's case, where her Future Self told her to wait for the job to turn up. At other times, our Future Selves give us specific instructions as to what to we might do, either literally or symbolically.

A good example of this comes from my own experience of writing this book. On several occasions, I've had reason to consult with a Future Self as to how to go forward with it. My biggest problem is always being short on time – a problem familiar to many, no doubt. One day when the panic about not having enough time became too big a block, I set up a Future Progression to explore what was going on. The Future Self I met at first was a real puzzle. It initially presented as a large hard-edged cube, and seemed to be made from obsidian or jet. Either way, it came across as very resistant, with no give in it whatsoever. It just seemed to exude 'must' and 'should'. As I looked at it, it resolved slowly into a rather hard-nosed looking businessman, sitting behind a large desk. He was immaculately dressed in an expensive suit and a crisp white shirt and dark tie. Everything about him seemed polished, even his head, which was completely bald. He sat at his desk, looking straight at me, whilst tapping his left hand impatiently on the desk. I noticed a very expensive watch on his wrist. As the silence went on, I realised I was feeling very intimidated and sensed I was about to be disciplined. It was quite clear that I wasn't to speak first.

After what felt like an eternity, he shifted in his chair and spoke. He said he'd called this meeting because I needed to be told a few things, principally that I couldn't write this book. When I asked him why, he said it was because I didn't have a structure, and that was because I wasn't able to create a structure. I wasn't any good at it. I was only good at the journalism I wrote – 'the quick stuff', as he called it (for which I was clearly meant to read 'shallow' and 'superficial'). I wasn't enough of a heavyweight to write this book.

Panic washed over me. Here, now, in this present time, I'd signed contracts. I had to deliver. What if he was right and I couldn't do this? Fortunately, I was aware enough to realise what was happening here. Part of the present me did think this was true. I was talking to a potential Future Self that I didn't want to be, but that I could create, if I allowed myself to believe what I was hearing. So I thanked him and came back to my convergence point. But puzzlingly, before I did, he gave me a pair of cuff-links, because he said I'd need them.

Back at the convergence point, I refocused and asked to meet the Future Self who wrote the version of this book that was published and did well. This time, I met a smiling woman wearing a soft-textured teal blue jacket over a flowery dress with a handkerchief hem. Curiously, she was wearing ballet shoes and kept tip-toeing about in them. She lost no time in telling me all I had to do was focus, be precise, and tread lightly. I was to stop worrying about time, as I had enough. Panicking would only use up time and energy and get in my creative way. She then gave me a clock face, cut into twelve segments. I now had time. And that's where the session ended.

Once I resurfaced, I realised the images and energies I'd

encountered had given me a lot to think about. A comparison of the two Future Selves produced a lot of insight. The first Future Progression was a little unnerving, since it suggested that I was capable of creating a future where I felt 'less than' – less than capable; less than was needed; less than I ought to be. All the details of the image pointed to that. I felt judged by this powerful, successful man as seriously lacking in what it took to produce a good book. I was taking too much time (hence the emphasis on the tapping hand with its expensive wrist watch) and didn't have the ability to put it together properly (hence his immaculate appearance and surroundings).

As I reflected on these images, I realised he was right in that most of my writing experience was journalistic, which, by necessity, tends to be fast and short. But did that necessarily mean I was incapable of taking on a book?

The alternative Future Self thought differently. Her gentler approach was reflected in her clothing, especially its colour and style. And, of course, the ballet shoes also made their point, so to speak. Be precise, and tread lightly. In other words, don't get bogged down. If I only had one day free for writing, I wasn't to tell myself I *only* had a day. I needed to change my attitude. I needed to tell myself I had a *whole* day and remind myself how much I could accomplish with that. That's why she gave me the clock, cut into segments. It was her way of telling me that I needed to deal with things in segments. That way, there would be time for everything that needed to be done.

So, unsurprisingly, I opted for the ballet shoes and the clock, metaphorically speaking. Oh, and I mustn't forget the cuff-links, which turned out to be very important. On reflection, I realised that what my businessman had given me, intimidating though he was, was a symbolic means of linking things, so that they held together. What he'd helped me realise was that a book is a series of sections, held together by a core idea – the cuff-links. The writing of the book became easier after this.

Health Issues

Another area that Future Progression can help with is health. Never to be used as a substitute for proper medical advice and treatment, it can nevertheless be of considerable help in terms of providing insight into what's given rise to an ailment and where it might go, as well as what might help in its treatment.

Again, a personal story provides a good illustration of how this works – or rather, in this case, how not to do it. A few years ago, I'd reached a point where I wasn't feeling my usual energetic self. I knew it was nothing serious; I was just not operating at 100% and feeling heavy and sluggish. I decided to check it out using my usual imagery approach. Entering my inner world, I was surprised to find myself on the pages of a Thomas the Tank Engine book, talking to The Fat Controller. For those not acquainted with the Rev Awdry's delightful children's stories, he writes about the lives of a little locomotive called Thomas and his friends, whose work and maintenance are organised by, amongst others, a rather officious character called The Fat Controller. Complete with top hat and tailcoat, and clutching his clipboard, he was insistent that I needed more regular maintenance and that I should give more thought to the fuel I was using, because otherwise I'd be storing up trouble for myself in the future, and I'd end up not being able to leave the engine shed.

I took what he was saying on board – or so I thought. I carried on with my hectic schedule, travelling all over the country running workshops, doing radio, giving lectures, carrying out consultations and writing. Ideal though this lifestyle wasn't, I thought I was looking after myself. So well was I *not* doing this that I eventually ended up in hospital, being checked out for what initially was thought to be a heart attack, but proved not to be. Eighteen months of excruciating pain later and after much medical head-scratching, I was found to have gall-stones and an infected gall bladder, which had started to impact on my liver. Their removal involved a four and a half hour operation and it took me six months to recuperate. The Fat Controller had been right. He represented those organs in my body that *control the digestion of fat* – my liver and gall bladder. I'd needed regular maintenance (I should have had regular check-ups) and I'd needed to watch the 'fuel' I was using, as in the quality and quantity of the food I'd been eating – always difficult to do when you're travelling. I hadn't, and I'd ended up not being able to leave the engine shed.

Was this encounter with the Fat Controller a Future Progression? Strictly speaking, probably not, but he was being predictive. He knew what was likely to happen if I didn't change what I was doing. If I'd applied what I teach, I'd have met a Future Self to explore this more and to ask for advice on how I could best prevent myself being stuck in the loco shed.

Pay Attention to the Details

As I've described how we can use Future Progression at a personal level, you'll have noticed that I've included a lot of detail about the images that occurred, including things like the colours they were wearing, items they might have been carrying, the expressions on their faces, the tone of voice used, and so on. Noticing the details really pays off, which is why it's a good idea to reflect on them for a while. They can yield deep insights. Symbolically, they not only tell the story and describe the problem, but so often supply the solution. My problems with time were illustrated by my businessman's finger-tapping impatience and his expensive wristwatch, for example. An answer to my problem was symbolically suggested by the ballet shoes my alternative Future Self was wearing – tread lightly, keep to 'the point' and stay focused. She reinforced her 'point' by giving me a clock. But another answer was also supplied in the form of the cuff-links my businessman gave me. It would have been very easy to miss or dismiss that small detail, which would have been to miss the helpful realisation that I was able to create structure by building around a core idea.

Claire's Gold Star, Maureen's Fairy Self, Linda's lonely forest, my Fat Controller – all these images convey something about the situation and carry some idea of a solution. The more you reflect on them, the more information they're likely to yield, so it's really worth giving time to them. But it's also important to remember that these insights are *guidance messages*. They're not once-and-for-all solutions or panaceas for all ills. Don't do what Donald did and imagine that you only have to do this once. This kind of work is meant for the journey. You use it time and time again to help you make better choices, find the right direction.

Chapter 7

Using Your Future for Business

At the time of writing, the Great Credit Crunch that began in earnest in 2008 has us in its jaws and is threatening to chew us up and swallow us. Whilst I think the media is giving us a distorted impression of what's really happening, we are facing undeniable problems. But if you'll forgive my mangling of Dylan Thomas' poem, we do not have to go gentle into that good night. The light isn't dying. It's changing. And dying or changing, raging against it won't be particularly constructive. What's needed is a different approach, one that working with your Future Self can provide.

If you're facing redundancy, repossession, bankruptcy, or anything else that looks like a disaster, hold hard. Make a deliberate point of putting your fear on one side and consult your Future Self. Apart from anything else, working with your Future Self helps you get a handle on what's really going on, globally as well as for you personally. And that awareness helps us to go about things differently. I do have some idea of what I'm talking about here, because I lost my house in the last recession and had five children to bring up on £60 a week, a situation which required considerable inventiveness.

Redundancy/Losing Your job

You may be one of the fortunate who wanted to give up work anyway. You have enough to live on, and you just needed the push. If so, you can skip this section.

But what if you've lost a job you liked or, just plain and simple, needed in order to pay the bills and you need to find another way of earning a living fast? Well, before you rush out there and take just anything, take half an hour to talk to your Future Self.

Questions you might consider asking are:

- *What are you, my Future Self, doing three or five years ahead?*
- *What are you, my Future Self, able to tell me about why this has happened to me? What's it teaching me/showing me?*
- *What do I do now? Or rather, what was the first step you took when you, my Future Self, were where I am now?*

Everything I said about fear in the last chapter is even more relevant here. Fear can derail us, if we let it. You can prevent fear paralysing you by asking questions like the ones above and then acting on the answers you get. Don't try and pretend you're not afraid. Instead, turn your fear into a motivator. Use it to get you to move, to get you to think, to get you to act. Go through the relaxation process and then find the Future Self that took the best course of action.

An up-to-the-minute and highly relevant example of how to use Future Progression in a business context comes from the experience of a business client of mine. Richard was a company director of a sizeable firm of estate agents. He was increasingly worried by the policy decisions his fellow directors were making in the face of the stalled housing market, because he believed them to be driven by fear and all he could see was disaster ahead if they persisted with their approach. After exploring the situation with his Future Self, he decided to resign from the company and set up his own estate agency business on a completely different basis. From a rational perspective, this was a mad move. But it's working. He regularly checks in with his Future Self and, as of now, he's the one estate agent I know who's doing really well, selling houses and meeting his own set targets – no mean feat, in view of the current market.

Setting Up or Developing Your Business

This might seem like a bonkers time to set up a business. But if you've lost your job, this might actually be the ideal time to do it. Yes, it'll involve risk and effort, but you'll have the help of your Future Self on tap.

This is an area where Future Progression really comes into its own. There are two ways that you can ask about your business and how to go about setting it up and/or developing it. The first is the usual way of asking your Future Self how s/he went about it. Set up a business meeting in your internal world. Ask your Future Self how s/he went about taking the business forward. Ask detailed questions. Yes, I know you want to know if it's successful, but if this 'meeting' is going to be of any use, you want to know in detail HOW your Future Self made it successful. Treat your Future Self like a good business consultant. And don't forget that crucial question: when your Future Self was where you are now, what was the first thing s/he did? That'll tell you what you need to be doing now. As always, don't settle for vagueness. Push for detail; make a pest of yourself. Your Future Self is there to help you, remember, so make it clear that you won't accept lofty condescension or mystical mutterings. You want answers.

Also, be realistic. You're in business. You've a product or a service you want to sell. So ask for realistic guidance. Ask your Future Self for help with marketing and PR; ask for help with finding funding; ask for help with increasing your turnover; ask for help with finding the right people to work for you. What did your Future Self do when s/he needed a loan? How did s/he approach the bank manager with the new business expansion plan? How did s/he put together the new business plan? You want detail, honest, down-to-earth detail. One of the biggest problems people create for themselves is that they often think spiritual and material can't work together when, actually, the spiritual underpins everything.

In my role as a business coach, I've met many people who thought it was wrong to ask for bog-standard everyday material help from spiritual sources, and it's come as a real shock to them to realise that they could. I believe that you can't separate the spiritual from the material, that the spiritual informs and underpins all else – a concept often referred to as the *immanence* of the divine, that is, the *indwellingness* of the spiritual in all things. This idea is far from new and has, in fact, been embraced by spiritual thinkers for millennia. For me, it's particularly well expressed by the approach of the mediaeval English mystic, Mother Julian of Norwich. Ensconced in her little hut adjoining Norwich Cathedral, she would dispense advice to the many people of all sorts and conditions who would come to her for help and guidance. As part of that guidance, she would be as likely to talk to you about the condition of your bowels as she was about the state of your spirit, as she saw no separation between the material and the spiritual, indeed believing that the one informed and shaped the other. She was a spiritual realist, which is what you'll need to be in business.

Other Business Uses
Is this the right job for me?
If you're not sure if a career is for you, you can 'try it on'. Ask to meet your Future Self from three or five years ahead in that role. The way your Future Self presents will tell you whether or not that job is for you.

Amanda recently did just this when she wanted to find out whether she really wanted to be a veterinary nurse. She'd always loved animals, and thought that she'd be good in a role of that kind. She asked to meet the Future Self who went down that route and was very surprised to meet up with an old lady with a curly blue rinse perm wearing a twin set! Remembering what I'd said about the Future Self being symbolic, she realised this wasn't her literal self and went ahead and asked her whether she'd trained for that job, and how she'd got on. The old lady said that she'd started it, but realised that she couldn't cope with the animals being in such pain, and had instead gone for another job. She'd then done voluntary work in a local animals' charity shop in her spare time. Amanda asked her what the other job was, but Twin Set Lady told her that she would have to meet another Future Self to find that out.

Reflecting on what she'd discovered, Amanda realised that her Future Self represented that gentle (possibly even genteel) part of her that wouldn't have been able to deal directly with animal suffering. She'd be much better off channelling her love of animals into a different way of helping them, hence the suggestion of voluntary work. She explored her way forward with another Future Progression, this time meeting a Fairy Godmother character who told her that she'd been offered a job with a housing association. She'd taken it and was now happily settled in that role. Amanda is now in a 'watch this space' position, carrying on with her current job in retail while she looks for a suitable vacancy with a housing association.

Whilst this is an unfinished story, it was still helpful in that it enabled Amanda to distinguish between what she'd like to do and what she was able to do in reality. It saved her from making a false start and then having to undo all her plans, as well as unnecessary expenditure on training courses and a possible move.

Recruitment

Future Self work can be helpful on the other side of the desk, too. If you're responsible for employing staff, you can save yourself a lot of hassle by talking to the Future Self who employed the candidate in question and asking how it turned out. I'm not suggesting for one minute that you make your decision based only on what your Future Self has to say, but you can use it as part of your deliberations.

Once you've invited the Future Self who employed that particular candidate, the first thing to do is notice how that Future Self looks – Calm? Energised? Harassed? That in itself can tell you something about how things turned out. Then ask how the job candidate is doing. Your Future Self is likely to tell you, maybe literally, maybe symbolically. Just don't be too swift to judge. Your Future Self may show you a picture of the candidate as a tortoise, for example. Don't jump to conclusions. Ask your Future Self what this image means. S/he may say that yes, the person is slow, but painstaking, with an eye for detail and that may be just the quality needed for the job in question. As always, pay attention to the details in your images and ask questions, to make sure you've got the right message.

Kathy was looking for a manager for her restaurant, and was seriously considering one of the candidates – a young woman with a bright smile and an engaging nature. She decided to check it out with her Future Self and was a bit puzzled when her Future Self just showed her a colour to represent the candidate. She didn't like the colour much, because it was a kind of sludgy maroon. Wondering what on earth this had to do with her questions about whether to employ the woman or not, Kathy asked her Future Self what it meant. Her Future Self shrugged and asked Kathy how she felt looking at the colour. She thought about it and realised she felt pulled down and depressed. Her Future Self told her to follow through on that and so, wondering if this represented something about her favoured candidate, Kathy checked up with her past employer and found out that she'd taken a lot of time off work on account of depression and associated health problems and that, in fact, had been the reason she'd left her previous job. Although she sympathised with the girl's plight, Kathy realised she needed to employ someone she could rely on. She went back to her Future Self and asked to be shown the candidate who'd best fit her requirements, and employed the one who was shown surrounded by sunflowers.

Working with your Future Self in this way can stop you making some bad choices, although it can work in some curious ways. For some time now, I've been consulting my Future Self about employing clerical help, only to have her (an elderly but energetic hair-rollered cleaning lady in a cross-over apron) tell me (whilst brandishing a mop) that now's not the time to employ anyone, and to get on with it myself, much to my disgruntlement. I live in hope.

These are just some of my suggestions as to how you can get your Future Self to work for you. But don't stop here. Be creative. Consult your Future Self about any aspect of your job or business, alongside your regular advisers.

Talking to the Spirit of the Business

All things have what I've come to call an Essential Spirit – even businesses. They exist as entities in their own right. I first discovered this many years ago, when I worked with a friend who owned a Mind Body Spirit shop, the spirit of which I talked to on her behalf on many occasions. I usually sensed it as a column of white light. The spirit of the business would tell me what it wanted done and how to go about it, and I'd pass that information on to my friend, and she'd put it into action. The advice often took the form of practical input, such as suggestions as to what courses to offer, what events to run, what kind of stock to buy, even how to dress the window. The business flourished, bringing help and guidance to many, in part, I like to think, because we listened to the business itself. Since then, I've learned to talk to the Essential Spirit of other businesses, including my own. From there, it was a short step to learning how to talk to the Future Business. It's not very different from talking to a Future Self. You call on the Spirit of the business in its future form from as many years ahead as you wish to go. Unsurprisingly, it usually appears in symbolic form. You can then talk to it about how it developed, what worked, what didn't, what you need to avoid.

An early example from my own experience led me to encounter my Future Business as a magical lighthouse, sending out its beams of light all round the world. As I watched, people started walking in along the beams of light, initially a few at a time, their numbers increasing until there were hundreds, then thousands of people walking in on those beams. I realised as I watched that I was being shown that in time, I'd be connecting with many thousands of people, and understood that I'd end up working through the media – which is exactly what's happened.

What I failed to take account of was that lighthouse keepers are usually one-man bands. They do the work on their own – all of it. I like to think that I'd have picked up on that if I'd given myself more time to consult with the image and, in retrospect, would probably have asked if it were possible to have a team to work with, especially since there were so many people coming in on those beams. As it was, I didn't and have spent the last few years working on my own. As mentioned above, my Future Self, though harassed, has repeatedly told me it hasn't been the right time to bring in help, although quite why that's been the case I can't fathom. However, I've an inkling that it's about to change, because current future images have shifted to what I interpret as having a more 'team' feeling. They include bouquets of rich-looking flowers (becoming one of a bunch?) and repeated visions of the Essential Spirit of my business as the main monsters from the cartoon *Monsters Inc*. Now this last may seem puzzling, and I did indeed have to sit with it for some time before I decoded it, but eventually they all sat round me in my internal boardroom, telling me that the moral of their cartoon story was learning how to do things differently – and as a result, more successfully. My interest is piqued by the 'they-ness' of what they have to say. And, of course, I need to pay attention to how the cartoon monsters did things differently in the story, because I'm sure there's a message in there for me somewhere.

It's work in progress. We'll see where it leads. In the meantime, I'm going to sit down and watch *Monsters Inc* a few times – all in the interests of research, you understand.

How to Talk to the Essential Spirit of Your Business

Find a quiet place and time. Sit quietly and bring your attention inward, centring yourself, using steady, even breathing. Allow yourself to relax, gently bringing your awareness to where you might be holding tension in your body... relaxing your jaw ... noticing where your shoulders are. If they're up under your ears, then gently relax them ... feeling your arms and hands and fingers becoming heavier ...

[PAUSE]

Then gently bring your attention to your upper body ... noticing whether you're holding any tension around your ribcage and across your upper back ... and if you are, just use your breathing to gently let go ... feeling the muscles relax, and all the little ribs heaving a sigh of relief as they let go ...

[PAUSE]

Then gently bring your attention to your lower body ... again noticing if you're holding any tension in this area ... if you're clamping your tummy muscles ...and if you are, use your breath to breathe relaxation into this whole area ... feeling your tummy muscles and any tension in the small of your back gently relaxing ...

[PAUSE]

Then bring your attention to the big muscles in your thighs ... telling them they can rest and let go ... letting any tension in your knees just dissolve away ... and any knots of tension in your calf muscles just unravel ... feeling your feet and toes becoming warm and heavy as any tension in your ankles just evaporates ...

[PAUSE]

Just letting yourself sit quietly for a moment or two ... feeling yourself being supported by whatever you're sitting or lying on... giving yourself over to its support ... relaxing completely...

[PAUSE]

Now in this place of stillness, gently allow an image of a crossroads or a place where paths converge to form in your mind ... let it settle ... and then ask to be shown the path or road you need to travel along in order to encounter the energy of your Future Business in its best outcome ... one of the paths will make itself known ...

[PAUSE]

Propel your awareness along that road or path, asking to meet with your business in its most successful future form ... from three (or five) years ahead ... and watch now as an image of your business slowly starts to form up ahead ... an image of the essence of your business, an image of its Future Essential Spirit ... and remember, this can be anything – human, animal, cartoon character, mythical character ... let it be whatever it wants to be ... give it time to form as fully as it needs to ... feel its energy, its essence, see it coming up to you know, drawing closer and closer ...

[PAUSE]

Say hello to it ... and pay attention, notice the details of the image ... and now ask the questions you want answers to ... ask for the advice you're searching for ...

[PAUSE for as long as you need]

And now it's nearly time to bring this meeting to an end ... but before you go, there's one question you need to ask this entity ... what was the first thing that was done when your business was where it is now, back in [state current month and year]? ... What were the first steps that were taken to solve the problem currently facing the business, here and now, in [state month and year]? ... Did they solve the problem? ... If they didn't, what should have been done? ...

[PAUSE]

Allow images, words, thoughts and feelings to come to you, knowing that they're coming to you from the entity that is the spirit of your Future Business ... if something's not clear, ask for clarification ...

[PAUSE]

When you feel you have your answers, thank this entity for helping you, and then watch as it gradually dissolves back into its place in the future ... and now it's time to start to make your way back ... start to bring your awareness back into the room ... bringing yourself back up through the different levels of awareness ... slowly bringing yourself back into normal waking consciousness ... until you find yourself back here, now, in this room ... Welcome back.

Now write down what you heard and saw and experienced and spend some time reflecting on what occurred whilst you were in your internal world. The guidance it contains may be immediately obvious, or it may take some time to decode, in which case keep coming back to it until you've cracked it.

Problem Solving and Trouble Shooting

If your business runs into problems, you can use Future Progression to help find solutions. Once again, you can either talk to the Future You who sorted the problems out, or you can talk to the Future Essential Spirit of your business.

If you choose to talk to your Future Self, you go about it in exactly the same way as you would normally, with a slight variation. Set up a meeting in your internal world with the Future Self who successfully sorts the problems out *for the highest good of all concerned* and then ask your questions. As always, pay attention to the details. How does your Future Self look and feel? What guidance are you given? And remember the most important question: what did your Future Self do when s/he was where you are now? The answer to that is always key. Remember, you ask to meet with the Future Self who successfully solves the problem for the highest good of all concerned. You need to be aware that this may not result in the outcome you believe you want. You may be told the business has to close, for example. But remember, you're asking for guidance *at the level of highest good*, and if you are told the business closes, then ask what it's clearing the way for. Your Future Self will tell you, or else will guide you to another source of help.

If you choose to talk to the Future Spirit of the Business, use the format outlined above. Remember to be proactive in this inner journey. Ask questions, ask for guidance. Listen and watch closely; pay attention to detail. Take a long hard look at the image of your Future Business. What is it actually? Every picture tells a story. Even if it's only a wash of colour, it'll have something to say. Is the colour washed out? Bright? Dingy? If it's a more concrete image, does it look alive and energetic? Does it look sad, dejected? Does it look under-nourished? Notice how you feel as you look at it. That'll tell you something, too. What does it have to say to you? What does it need right now? Does it just need a new direction? And again, always ask that all-important question: what were the first steps taken when your business was where it is currently? Were they productive? Did they solve the problem? If they didn't, what needed to happen to sort the problem out?

Remember too, that you can use this technique to try out different futures and get a handle on how they feel. The more you practise, the better you will become at decoding the imagery and sensing the best course of action.

Chapter 8

Shaping the Future, to Make Your Present

In the last chapter, we saw how it's possible to talk to what is effectively the future energy of a business. Now, this idea can be extended to just about anything. You can use it to communicate with the future spirit of a relationship, for example, or a project, or even a yet-to-be-born baby. All you have to do is evoke the Future Spirit of whatever it is you want to explore in whatever symbolic form it wants to take and communicate with it.

As always, the rules for communicating remain the same. The quality of your communication depends on the quality of your questions. Remember, general questions generate general answers, so avoid vague questions such as 'Are you successful?' You want to know *how* that success was achieved, and was it worthwhile? Was it fulfilling? Were there other, better choices? And, again, don't ask closed questions. 'Did you (my book) get published?' is an example of a closed question, because all it invites is a 'yes' or a 'no' response. It doesn't invite the Future Energy of your book to expand on its answer, and you can end up asking a string of questions which could feel like an interrogation. You want the Future Energy to talk freely and without too much prompting, so ask open questions, such as, 'What happened then?' and give the Future Energy the opportunity to talk about its experiences.

How Do You Go About This?

Let's say that you want to explore the future of a relationship.

After going through the relaxation process, you invite the Future Spirit (or Energy) of the *relationship* to meet you (*not* the other person in it), specifying from how far ahead. As always, pay attention to what form it takes when it comes forward, because, as always, the form it takes will speak volumes. Be patient and let the image develop, just as Jasmine did when she wanted to explore what the future held for her relationship with a high-powered, high-flying businessman. She loved him, but didn't know whether she'd be able to cope with his lifestyle. He travelled a great deal on business, and lived a fast-paced life, surrounded by up-to-the-minute technology, both at work and at home. Jasmine liked life to be a little slower and simpler. So she called up an image of the Future Energy of the relationship. Her first vision was of a desert, which seemed to confirm her fears. But as she held the vision, she realised that in the middle of her desert was an oasis, warm and peaceful, and that her attention was being drawn by one of the palm trees, which was gently waving its fronds at her, and telling her, "I'm a calm palm, I'm a calm palm ...".

To begin with, she couldn't connect this image with her fear of the frenetic lifestyle she thought she might have to face with this man, until she heard the palm tree talking to her in a quiet, friendly way about how she was this man's oasis. The quiet peaceful life she cherished was important to him, too, or so the palm tree told her. Talking to her man afterwards, she found out that this was true. She didn't need to 'keep up' with him; he valued and needed her loving peacefulness, something that had been in short supply in his previous relationships. He wanted to be able to come home and just rest and relax with her after all his fevered running about.

What if you want to explore the likely future of a project you're thinking of undertaking? Summon the Future Spirit of it, and talk to it. And what if that 'future project' happens to be having a baby? You can talk to the Future Spirit of that child, as Wendy did. Mother to four children already, Wendy had a sense that there was another child 'waiting to come in', so to speak. She wasn't at all sure she wanted another baby, and spent a good deal of time in conversation with this 'Future Child' about the wisdom of going ahead and being born. He won out and Wendy went ahead and gave birth to him – a fact she's extremely happy about. That's one young man with an interesting future ahead of him, I'd say.

Energy Shaping

It's possible to take this idea a step further.

Over the years, I've done a lot of research on manifesting – how to make things happen – and I discovered that we're in fact manifesting all the time. We're mostly just not conscious of it, which is why we often get things we don't want! Essentially, to manifest well involves learning how to work with energy in an appropriate way, and I put together a method called the Radial Technique[1] based on the principles I'd unearthed to help people do exactly that.

However, I also came to realise that manifestation and learning from the future had something in common. Manifesting was about making something happen that had yet to happen. Accessing the future was about working with a future event that had happened. What if I could somehow get in there in the middle and help bring the future into being by working on its energy? I experimented, to good effect, and so the idea of Energy Shaping was born.

It works on the basis that every created thing pre-exists in an energy form – whether it's an idea, a project, a painting or a Fair Isle sweater – and it's possible to engage with it in its future *energy* form *and improve on it* before it's made manifest. This can speed up the creative and constructive process considerably AND produce good results – an approach also supported by Gill Edwards in her book, Stepping Into the Magic[2] and Dina Glouberman in Life Choices, Life Changes.[3]

Let me give you an example. When I was studying for my Psychology degree, I was also a full-time parent with a three-quarters-time job. No surprises, then, that I was always pushed for time when it came to studying. Every six weeks or so, I'd have to read up for and write a 2000+ word assignment on a set topic. With the other demands on my time, I'd usually find myself with just 24 hours to get all this done. Given that kind of pressure, I knew I needed to do something Harry Potterish, if I was going to have a hope of producing anything. So I experimented with meeting the assignment in its future form before I even attempted to start on it literally. I learned how to tap into its energy and work on it 'energetically'. I'd evoke the essential spirit of the assignment and meet it in its as-yet unformed state, which could present as anything from a shapeless wash of colour to an unfinished cartoon figure with watery lines that kept moving, to an unfinished garden with plants that kept jumping about. Mostly, it would present as energy shapes – lights and colours that kept moving in and out of my (inner) vision. My task would be to pour into these images my intentions for the project. As I focused my consciousness on them, the lights and colours would start to steady and become more concrete. Once I felt satisfied with the images, I'd imagine absorbing them into myself. And then I'd start on the assignment, beginning with the reading I needed to do and then I would start to type, just letting the words flow from my brain through my fingers and onto the keys of the computer.

Unless some major family or domestic event intervened, I'd get that assignment in on time, every time. That in itself was amazing. But the truly remarkable thing would be that I'd usually get high marks, in the 80-90 per cent range, whenever I used this approach. And perhaps even more startling still, I had good recall of the material, and still do, eleven years on. I came to call this technique 'Energy Shaping', because that's what it felt like – shaping energy. I realised I could use it in all kinds of creative work, especially when I was under pressure, and I've since used it to help create workshops, articles and talks. Even this book has benefited, or so I'd like to think. When I first encountered it, it was a shapeless, blobby mass of watery white colour – a bit like the uncooked white of an egg. 'Eugh,' I thought, 'needs a bit of work.' So I focused on it, and beamed into it my desire and intention to create a good book, one that would sell well because it meant something to people, because I'd done a good job. This energy helped to tone up the white until it became a more solid flow of what looked like liquid marble, with white and grey swirls intertwining with crystalline sparkly bits. After that, the book seemed more graspable to me, and I went on to take the later advice of the lady in ballet shoes mentioned in Chapter Five to work on it chapter by chapter.

When I first discovered this approach, I'll admit I wasn't too keen on revealing it to my fellow students at the time, especially the ones who laboured over their assignments for weeks – not out of selfishness, but out of fear that they'd lynch me. I've taught it to many students of my own, however, with some outstanding results. Many have applied it to academic work, as I did. Others have used Energy Shaping for all kind of creative projects – writing, painting, as well as business projects and creating workshops and training courses.

How to Energy Shape

Sit or lie comfortably in a place where you won't be interrupted for at least 30 minutes. Have some water and a pen and some paper to hand. Focus on what it is you want to manifest; it could be an essay, a project of some kind, a design, whatever.

And now begin by focusing on your breathing ... just gently noticing the rise and fall of your breath ... its gentle movement in and out ... its ebb and flow ... and just allow yourself to relax ... letting your shoulders drop ... gently shifting your neck so that it sits comfortably on your spine ... feeling your arms and hands and fingers becoming warm and heavy ...

[PAUSE]

Feel yourself drifting ... as though you've become a feather, floating on the air ... imagine that you're a feather, leaning back on the support of the air, being carried hither and yon ... drifting in spirals, up and up, until you feel you've crossed over into another place, another dimension... crossing over what's known as the Paradox Line, where the outer world becomes your inner world ...

[PAUSE]

Now, just use your awareness to explore this place out of time that you find yourself in ... and become aware that somewhere near you is the energy that is your project ... it's in its pre-form state ... just allow yourself to connect with it, to recognise it, to know it ... and allow yourself to sense or see what state it's in ...

[PAUSE]

Now focus on it ... and pour into it all your intention for it ... that it be accurate, that it be beautiful, that it be helpful, that it be useful, that it be what it should be, in all its perfection ... if it's a book, intend that it be of service to those who need it ... if it's a training course, intend that it helps people to grow ... if it's a design project, intend that it communicates clearly and truthfully to those who see it ... whatever it is that you're working on, just pour into it all your best desires and intentions for it, asking that it be for the highest good of all concerned ... ask that it be what it needs to be ... and watch or sense as the energy shapes itself, aligns itself with your intentions ... perhaps the light becomes brighter, or the colours deepen, or it concretises into some kind of image ...

[PAUSE]

Now hold the image it has become in your awareness ... let yourself really sense it ... and then imagine it travelling towards you, coming closer and closer, until it starts to merge with you ... feel yourself absorbing this energetic image ... until it rests within you comfortably ...

[PAUSE]

If it doesn't settle, if it feels uncomfortable, bring the image back outside you and work a little more on it until you feel satisfied with what you achieve ... and then absorb the image once more, taking it into your heart or wherever feels comfortable ...

[PAUSE]

And now become aware of being the feather once more, and begin to drift back down to earth ... slowly bringing yourself back down and down, until you come back into your body, and can feel the chair you sitting on, or the floor you're lying on ... and can hear the sounds of daily life around you once more ...

Welcome back. Now take a sip of water and perhaps make some notes on your experience. You're ready to start on your project!

Notes and References

1. Hykel Hunt, M, **Your Manifesting Tool-kit: techniques for making things happen** (in preparation) *The Radial Technique* © is one of the manifesting techniques I teach. See workshops programme at www.hykelhunt.co.uk
2. Edwards, Gill, (2006) **Stepping into the Magic**, Piatkus Books
3. Glouberman, Dina, (2004) **Life Choices, Life Changes**, Mobius

Chapter 9

Imagine…

There's an Indian proverb that describes the human being as a house with four rooms – mental, physical, emotional and spiritual. To be on our way towards wholeness, this proverb says, we need to visit these rooms once a day, even if it's only to open the door to give them an airing.

I first came upon this proverb nearly 20 years ago, and it triggered an idea for an exploratory exercise I could use with my clients. I call it the 'House with Four Rooms'[1] and it's turned out to be a very powerful technique for helping people deepen their self-awareness.

I get my client to stand on a large sheet of A1 paper that has been divided into four quarters. These four quarters represent the 'four rooms' of their life – their mental, physical, emotional and spiritual aspects. First off, I ask the client to estimate how much time s/he thinks s/he spends in each 'room', as a percentage of the day. Unfortunately, the answers I've received to this question would suggest there's some truth in gender stereotypes, as men often report they spend most time in the mental/physical rooms, while women seem to spend more time in the emotional/mental, with physical trailing behind. I then ask them to step into each quadrant, one at a time, and to imagine as they do so that they're stepping into a room that represents each aspect, and to describe it to me. What they say reveals a great deal about how they function in each area. One woman, for example, was surprised to discover that her emotional room was a damp old basement where the laundry was done. There was mould on the walls and damp washing everywhere, not all of it hers. It alerted her to the possibility that she was 'taking in everyone's dirty washing' and that maybe she should do something about it.

Most people have few problems with imaging their mental, physical and emotional rooms and come up with rich and telling imagery that helps enormously with developing their self-awareness and uncovering blind spots, amongst other things. But the most telling room is often the Spiritual Room. Not only is this generally the room least visited on a daily basis, but the imagery is often stereotypical and lifeless. Churches crop up a lot, as do angels and wizards. Their stereotypical nature wouldn't be a problem if they were living images with some meaning and relevance to the person, but they so often aren't. It's so often just something that the client's come up with as 'something spiritual' to satisfy my questions.

My point in mentioning this is to illustrate the degree of unconscious spiritual poverty and hunger I encounter out there in the so-called real world. And this is as applicable to the shapers of our world as to us ordinary people. I often speculate what might be possible if politicians, bankers, CEOs, generals, scientists, makers and shapers of every kind, were in the habit of visiting their Spiritual Rooms in some way on a daily basis. And what might emerge if they were to get into the habit of consulting their Future Selves?

Just imagine …

What if bankers and financiers could have 'learned from the future' before we got into our current mess? They could have consulted with their Future Selves as to whether the 'creative products' they were selling would work. It begs the question as to whether they'd have changed anything, but at least there might have been some insight into what the future would hold. As it stands, no one had a clue about what was likely to ensue as a result of what BBC Business Editor Robert Peston calls the 'Turkey Twizzler' approach to financial products, where loans (good and bad) were so minced together that no banking corporation could tell what they were buying. If approached properly, perhaps their Future Selves could have helped them design better products in the first place, which might, in turn, have prevented the world being pitched in to its present recession.

Now that we ARE in recession, and facing major government spending cuts, not just in the UK but worldwide, what might be the result if our decision makers spent some time learning from the future? With the kind of squeeze on public spending that we're about to face, some crucial choices are going to have to be made, of what's known in the business world as the 'shoot the puppy' kind – that is, we're going to have to think the unthinkable and then do it. Libraries, museums, the arts are all areas that are likely to be seen as expendable. Drastic cuts will have to be made elsewhere in education, the NHS, local services. Things that have hitherto been thought of as sacrosanct – pensions and State benefits, for example – will be likely to be 'revised' – indeed, already have been in Ireland, where even Child Benefit has been reduced

At the time of writing, governments world-wide face huge decisions, far-reaching in their consequences, as they attempt to deal with the huge deficits generated by the financial debacle of 2008. What kind of thinking is going to go into these decisions? History suggests it will have a logical/rational basis. But what might the future suggest? What if our global decision makers dared to take a mental detour to learn from the future? Might the results not be more creative and sustaining? It could be an opportunity for positive change, a new approach to business and politics, enabling the development of what Danar Zohar calls *spiritual capital* through the addition of moral and social dimensions to the conduct of business and politics, giving rise to a kind capitalism that 'nourishes and sustains the human spirit as well as making business sustainable.'[2] What kind of world might we live in if our decision makers dared to learn from the future?

Let's take this into even more contentious territory. What if Tony Blair had consulted his Future Self over the matter that was to haunt his term of office, the invasion of Iraq? Would he have done anything differently? If Gordon Brown had been acquainted with the idea of talking to his Future Self, would he have been so keen to be Prime Minister? And let's really think the unimaginable: imagine George Bush exploring his role in the world's future before he stood for President. What might the outcome have been? And what if Barack Obama were in the habit of consulting his Future Self? What might be the results?

What if the delegates of the UN were to employ Future Self consultation on a regular basis, to explore the possible futures likely to result from different policies and decisions? Even if they didn't believe they were accessing the future, it could be a valuable exercise in blue-sky thinking. What if techniques such as *Learning from the Future* were deployed to explore ways in which the wounded people and places of the world could be helped and healed?

And what might we discover is possible with regard to global-warming if we adopted a *Learning from the Future* approach? Would new technologies be created earlier? What other discoveries might be found – and what courses of action decided against?

In anticipation of the charge likely to be levelled at me at this point, I don't believe this is a naïve approach. Rather, I think this shift in thinking that combines intellect and intuition is being daily made essential by the way our world is going. The *Learning from the Future* approach combines intellect and intuition and makes it possible to come up with sound, robust ideas that work, because they're based on a whole-brained approach.

It's customary for this kind of approach to be dismissed as dingley-dangley gobbledegook, the province of New Agers, as Hillary Clinton discovered when she dared to try out a new way of thinking back in the nineties. She hit the headlines because she did some psycho-spiritual work with world famous 'geologian' Jean Houston,[3] which involved her talking in her imagination to one of the people she most admired, namely Eleanor Roosevelt. This isn't a particularly weird technique – it's an imaginative visualisation exercise often used in coaching circles and Gestalt therapy, designed to access insights and answers from the unconscious. But that's not what the American press thought when they got hold of this tasty bit of news. 'Hillary Clinton conducts séance!' screamed the headlines, killing off any possibility that a creative and whole-brained approach might have found its way into the White House, at that time at any rate.

But I still hope. I'd like to think that *Learning from the Future* could be used to make a difference from the top down, but I'm not going to wait for that. The good thing about *Learning from the Future* is that it can be used to change things from the bottom up, at the level of the individual. Yes, we can use it to help ourselves. But I believe we can also use it to help bring about change for the wider good. We can work in groups and singly to explore the way to go, and if enough of us do it or techniques like it, it will filter out and up, effecting change in the global consciousness.

How might we do this? Let me give an example drawn from my own experience. A short while ago, a group I regularly work with called *Intuition@Work*[4] decided to use the *Learning from the Future* method for insight into the current world economic situation – what had caused it, what it was really about and what we could do about it, personally and globally. We sat together but carried out the visualisation individually. As I began to shift state, the image of the character Faramir from the *Lord of the Rings* kept coming into my head. I kept pushing it away, because I thought it was just 'noise round the signal' and tried to clear the way for other images to come in. But it persisted, and so in the end, I gave in and focused on him. The image immediately dissolved and instead I found myself looking at the Master Ring that was the cause of all the trouble in that story. It suddenly dawned on me that, of course, it was a *tainted* ring, made from toxic energies and designed to gain control over the entire world. That's what lay at the root of the whole problem in the story – greed for power that had resulted in corrupted gold, both in Tolkien's story and in what was going on – and still is – in our world. As an image for what was happening globally in the world of finance, it was an effective symbol. Tainted gold was damaging us all.

And the analogy symbolised our present crisis more widely. In Tolkien's story, the course of the future is dictated by how the archetypal characters in the tale respond to the Ring. Although initially tempted, Faramir resists the lure of the Ring in the end and indirectly helps to bring about its destruction, thereby helping the world return to a state of peace and sustainable values – unlike his brother, Boromir, who is consumed by desire for the Ring and meets his death as a consequence. Decoding the imagery, I realised that Boromir represented the continuance of the old ways of reacting, and Faramir represented doing things differently. Boromir's fate shows us that 'more of the same' isn't the answer. We need to 'do a Faramir' and resist the lure of that tainted gold, because all it has done and will do is bring about the eventual destruction of everything around us, right down to the earth we stand on.

If that's the problem, I thought, what do we need to do about it? What does our response need to be? For an answer to this, I decided to meet the Spirit of the Future from ten years ahead – not my own Future Self, but the Spirit of the World from that time ahead. The imagery I encountered surprised me, to say the least. The energy of the 'best possible future' was embodied as a typical woman from the 1950s, complete with immaculate perm, bright red lipstick, high-heeled shoes and a classic fifties wide-skirted dress with a frilly apron over the top. She put me in mind of a rather glamorous home economics demonstrator, especially as she was wielding a wooden spoon.

Looking at her, I was puzzled. I seemed to have gone back, not forward, and said so. She was instantly quite cross with me.

'I'm not the past. I'm the future,' she said irritably. 'I'm here to tell you that you've all created this mess through sheer greed and you need to get a grip on what frugality means. Being frugal doesn't mean being stingy. It means using your resources wisely. All of them.' All of this was accompanied by some very dogmatic spoon pointing. 'If you all start to practise proper frugality now, you'll come through. You'll not only come through, but you'll also have brought about some much-needed changes in basic attitudes, too. It doesn't mean you can't still have the good things in life. It just means you'll have to learn to wait a little longer and plan and budget and be creative with what you've got – No more spending non-existent money; no more borrowing from your children's future.'

And then she vanished, and all I could hear in my head was the theme tune from the film *Titanic*. Very comforting, I thought, until I heard her voice saying, 'It's all right, you won't hit the iceberg this time.'

I'll admit I was puzzled by this imagery and I had to give a great deal of time over to thinking about it. A woman from the 1950s? What on earth was that all about? It certainly didn't sound too enlightened to me; a time of narrow-minded thinking, when everyone knew their place and was expected to stay in it; a time of hierarchies and class structure and racism; the 11+ that marked you for life, one way or another. My list of negatives was lengthy.

And then I began to realise that it had to be seen in context. The 1950s was a period when Britain was emerging from a time of darkness and fear. There was still rationing, but things were getting better. Compared with the way things had been for the last decade, it would have been a time of hope and gradual steadying and improvement – a time of greater security, when there was more to eat and spend. But the recent memories of lack and deprivation and fear would have brought with them an accompanying frugality. A good and proper frugality, focused on making good use of what one had, not just frittering it. I began to realise what Mrs 1950s had been saying. Being frugal didn't – doesn't – mean being mean and stingy and joyless. It meant – means – using everything we have as well as we can, as consciously as we can. It means not grabbing for more than we really need.

And we don't have to live a joyless life to do this. We've become wedded to the idea that things make us happy – the new kitchen, the new car, the new dress. But we're rediscovering what's been discovered by many generations before us over the millennia – that things by themselves don't make us happy; that things, and the pursuit of things, can make us very unhappy. We're discovering all over again the truth that Steinbeck was driving at when he wrote

We can stand anything God and Nature throw at us, save only plenty. If I wanted to destroy a nation, I would give it too much, and I would have it on its knees, miserable, greedy and sick.[5]

We can live contentedly, living frugally. Put another way, frugality means spending the energies of the present wisely, so that we don't spend the energies of the future, so that we save something for the future. My 1950's cookery demonstrator did have a thing or two to say, I discovered, and continues to, as I unearth new meanings in her symbolism, as is the way with all good image work.

But how can I make an impact 'out there' with what is, after all, very personal imagery, I asked myself? I found both comfort and inspiration in Danar Zohar's words. First quoting Jung's words,

> In our most private and subjective lives we are not only the passive witnesses of our age, its sufferers, but also its makers. We make our own epoch,[6]

she goes on to say,

> To live our lives on the scale of epoch making, it is not necessary to be president of the United States, CEO of a vast global enterprise, or even an aid worker in Africa. We just have to stay true to our own deepest ideals and values and make what difference we can at whatever level we operate in life.[7]

As ever, the change needs to begin with me. In being it, I can live it, model it, show it.

Let's learn from the future, by all means. But let's also remember that what we're looking for in our futures is that which improves and heals our present. That's its whole point.

Notes and References

1. I first heard of this proverb in Rumer Godden's autobiography, *The House with Four Rooms*, Corgi, 1990. The method I've created is called H4R©
2. Zohar, D, *Spiritual Capital*, (2005), Bloomsbury, London
3. For an example of Jean Houston's approach, see Houston, J, (1982), *The Possible Human*, Tarcher Press
4. *Intuition@Work* is an approach I devised to business coaching in 2005. See www.hykelhunt.co.uk for further details
5. Parini J,(1995), *John Steinbeck: A Biography*, Minerva, p504
6. Jung, C, *The Meaning of Psychology for Modern Man* in The

Collected works of C G Jung, Vol 10: Civilisation in Transition, (1953), RKP, London

7. Zohar, D, *ibid*, p 225-226

Appendix

Variation on the script for the Future Progression

As a variation to the cross-roads visualisation, you might like to try the *Hall of Doors* method, as follows:

Make yourself comfortable, sitting or lying down, and close your eyes. Remind yourself why you're doing this and what your questions are.

And now begin by focusing your attention on your breathing ... just focus on your breath, letting your breath gently rise and fall ... noticing the ebb and flow of your breath ... and, at the same time, give yourself permission to relax ... just checking through your body for where you might be holding tension ... letting your jaw soften ... noticing where your shoulders are, and if they're up underneath your ears, just let them relax, and let your arms and hands and fingers become heavy ...

[Pause]

And now just notice how you're holding your upper body ... if you're clamping your muscles around your ribs and shoulder blades, just use your breath to help them relax ... just breath ease and relaxation through your muscles ... letting your ribs relax, and feel each one of them give a little sigh of relief as they let go...

[Pause]

Allow yourself now to become aware of how you're holding your lower body, and again, if you're clamping your muscles around your tummy and lower back, just breathe through them, telling them they can let go for the time being ... and feel that girdle of muscles gently relaxing all the way round, across your

97

abdomen ... and around into the small of your back ...

[Pause]

And now gently bring your attention to the muscles in your legs ... relaxing the muscles in your thighs, just noticing how the rest of the muscles in your legs let go, too ... feel any tension you may be holding in your knees just evaporate ... and let any little knots of muscles in your calves gently unravel ... feeling any tension in your ankles just dissolve away ... leaving your feet and toes feeling warm and heavy ...

[Pause]

And now just allow yourself to sit there for a moment or two ... giving yourself over to the support of the chair or the floor ... feeling yourself being held up by the chair or the floor ... just give yourself over to their support, ... just ... letting ... go ...

[Pause]

Now just imagine that you're floating ... gently floating ... gently floating down, softly falling, just like Alice in Wonderland falling down the rabbit hole ... it's a pleasant experience ... just floating down ... until your feet touch the ground ... you gently open your inner eyes and look around ... and you realise you're standing in the middle of a vast circular hall, with a number of doors set in its ancient walls ... Notice how many doors there are and where they are in relation to you. Are they all in front of you? Are there any behind you? What do they look like? Are they old or modern? Large or small? What colour might they each be? Are they all the same, or are they different? Do they have any door handles? Just notice the details...

[Pause]

Now ask to be shown the door that will be of most benefit to you to explore beyond on this occasion. You will be drawn to one of the doors ...

[Pause]

And now imagine yourself opening that door and going

through it. What lies beyond? Is it a room? If so, what kind of room? An office? A ballroom? A cellar? Or do you find yourself in a landscape? If so, what kind of landscape? Open fields? A mountain top? A forest? Where do you find yourself? Is it night or day, summer or winter? Allow yourself to absorb the details. Notice, too, how you feel being here – are you happy to be here? Do you feel safe? Puzzled? Curious? Again, just accept the feelings you experience ...

[Pause]

Now, you see someone or something coming towards you. Let the image become clearer as this entity comes closer. You know this is your Future Self from ...... years hence, the Future Self who dwells in this dimension ... As the image draws closer, take in the details. Notice how your Future Self presents, because the imagery will have meaning...

[Pause]

And now your Future Self comes up and greets you, and you respond. This is your opportunity now to talk to your Future Self and to ask the questions you want answers to. Take as much time as you need to do this, allowing your Future Self sufficient time to respond as well, either in words or thoughts or pictures or symbols. If you're confused by anything your Future Self gives you, ask for clarification. Take as much time as you need...

[Pause]

Your time is drawing to a close ... but before this experience comes to an end, just take your consciousness, your awareness, your sense of yourself, and lift it out of you and drop it into your Future Self, so that you are looking back at your Present Self through your Future Self's eyes ... Notice what you see or feel as you look back at your Present Self ... how do you look? ... What do you need? ... Let your Future Self supply the answers to your awareness ... and then allow yourself to come back into your Present Self ...

[Pause]

And there's one more question you might like to ask. **Just ask your Future Self what she or he did when she or he was where you are now.** What was the first step she or he took when they were where you are right now? Allow yourself to hear or feel or sense or just know the answer ...

[Pause]

And now your Future Self has a gift for you ... a symbolic gift that will help you on your way ... again, just take the first image that comes into your head. It can be anything, so allow it to be what it needs to be. If you need more information about it, ask your Future Self to explain it ...

[Pause]

... And now it's time to say your farewells, so thank your Future Self for coming to see you ... and now just allow your Future Self to merge with you ... notice how you feel as he or she steps into you and just melds with you ... really allow yourself to feel this experience ...

[Pause]

And then come back through the door into the great hall, which represents your present and all its possibilities. Check whether you need to go through any of the other doors. If you do, just go through this new door as you did before and find yourself in whatever lies beyond... when it's time to return to everyday awareness, then just allow yourself to start coming back through the different levels of awareness, as though you're a diver, swimming back up slowly to the ocean's surface. Don't come up too fast ... take your time and surface slowly ... slowly coming back to everyday awareness, bringing back with you the memories of what you heard and felt and saw ... slowly surfacing ... until you feel ready to open your eyes ... and are ready to be back, present in this room, at this time, awake and refreshed.

Take a sip or two of water and then make notes on your experience.

Select Bibliography/Further Reading

Blackmore, Susan, (2003), *Consciousness: An Introduction*, Hodder and Stoughton

Carroll, Lewis, (2003), *Alice's Adventures in Wonderland: AND Through the Looking Glass*, Rev Edition, Penguin Classics

Carter, Rita, (2002), *Consciousness*, Weidenfeld and Nicolson

Chown, Marcus, (2007), *Quantum Theory Cannot Hurt You: A Guide to the Universe*, Faber and Faber

Davies, Paul, (2005), *About Time*, Paperback edition, Simon and Schuster

Edwards, Gill, (2006), *Stepping into the Magic*, Piatkus Books

Glouberman, Dina, (2004), *Life Choices, Life Changes: Develop your Personal Vision for the Life you want*, Mobius

Greene, Brian, (2004), *The Fabric of the Cosmos*, Penguin Books

Houston, Jean, (1982), *The Possible Human*, Tarcher Press

Kant, Immanuel, (2007), *Critique of Pure Reason*, Penguin Classics

Leibniz, G (1992), *Discourse on Metaphysics and other Essays*, Hackett Publishing

Libet, Benjamin, (2004), *Mind Time: The Temporal Factor in Consciousness*, Harvard University Press

McEvoy, J.P. and Zarate, O. (1996), *Quantum Theory for Beginners*, Icon Books

McTaggart, Lynne, (2003), *The Field*, Element Books

Radin, Dean, (2006), *Entangled Minds*, Paraview Pocket Books

Shroder, T (2001), *Old Souls: Scientific Search for Proof of Past Lives*, Simon and Schuster

Smedley, Jenny, (2006), *Souls Don't Lie: A True Story of Past Lives*, O Books

Weiss, Brian, (1994), *Many Lives, Many Masters: The True Story of a Prominent Psychiatrist, His Young Patient and the Past-life Therapy That Changed Both Their Lives*, Piatkus Books

Weiss, Brian, (2004), *Same Soul, Many Bodies*, Piatkus Books

White, T.H. (1996), *The Once and Future King*, Voyager
Zohar, Danah, (1991), *The Quantum Self*, Flamingo
Zohar, Danah, (2004), *Spiritual Capital: Wealth We Can Live By*, Bloomsbury

BOOKS

O is a symbol of the world, of oneness and unity. In different cultures it also means the "eye," symbolizing knowledge and insight. We aim to publish books that are accessible, constructive and that challenge accepted opinion, both that of academia and the "moral majority."

Our books are available in all good English language bookstores worldwide. If you don't see the book on the shelves ask the bookstore to order it for you, quoting the ISBN number and title. Alternatively you can order online (all major online retail sites carry our titles) or contact the distributor in the relevant country, listed on the copyright page.

See our website **www.o-books.net** for a full list of over 500 titles, growing by 100 a year.

And tune in to myspiritradio.com for our book review radio show, hosted by June-Elleni Laine, where you can listen to the authors discussing their books.

MySpiritRadio